"Scott's been my Everyday Poet for some years. Vivid and witty, the poems ride on a lyrical rhythm and celebrate life with a quiet sincerity."

- Eunji Lee

"I have known Scott Oury for years. I have never known anyone more dedicated to poetry. Read the poems silently and then aloud, on earth or on some cloud!"

- John Cutler Anderson

"I cherish the meditative quality and "peek into my heart" kind of fragile hope in these poems."

- Pete Jacobs

"I have read through the poems twice and found them clear, poetic, and often wise."

- David Cope, author of *A Musicianship Primer*

"At last! Since on special occasions I've heard some of Scott's poems read out loud, I have been holding my breath. Finally, here is his life's work. I love the range—from bringing to life the kid in all of us, "reaching high for hold," to the threat of nuclear disaster—in short the capacity to experience the breadth of life. Every poetry lover should have this book."

- Sally Kitt Chappell, author of *In Praise of Flesh*

"I've always been very selective about poetry, my interest being dependent upon the level of awareness a poet presents. Scott's insights are on a very high level, and across a wide range of human experience, something rarely encountered and to be greatly appreciated."

- Larry Borok

"Scott Oury is a gifted observer of the human condition, and story-teller of the lives he knew best. His views on politics, religion and environmental degradation are soulfully captured, often with humor. This friend, teacher, husband, father, sailor, and home-builder has shared hard-earned wisdom in New Moon by Half. He has lived fully, observed his world broadly, and shares his wisdom in simple, evocative language. Here is a gift to share within families, and with friends and colleagues, a gift that will prompt meaningful, illuminating conversations."

- Beth Ferguson

"Though I've been reading these poems over 30 years, an early poem, especially its first line, "I will have windows where I live," has stayed with me, and will remain with me until I take my last breath."

- Diane Saunders

New Moon
By Half

ALSO BY SCOTT OURY

Coming to Terms with Experience through Writing

New Moon By Half

A Lifetime in Poetry

SCOTT OURY

Copyright © 2019 Scott Oury

All rights reserved. No part of this publication may be reproduced, distributed, or transmitted in any form or by any means, including photocopying, recording, or other electronic or mechanical methods, without the prior written permission of the publisher, except in the case of brief quotations embodied in critical reviews and certain other noncommercial uses permitted by copyright law.

Printed and bound in the United States of America.

Grateful acknowledgement is made to the following for reprint permissions:

Law & Order Magazine,"To Valentine Vaduga Upon Complaint No. 628-0207," (October 1974)

HIS Magazine, "Corelli: Adagio at Christmas," (December, 1974)

Cover design by Jae Diego. Cover photo by Kym MacKinnon.

ISBN-13: 978-0-578-43370-7
Library of Congress Control Number: 2018911313

For Glynn, astute editor, wife, friend, and encourager—over long hours and years.

CONTENTS

FLESH AND BLOOD

PSYCHE

FAMILY

CHRISTIANITY

PERSONS

FRIENDS AND LOVERS

GLYNN

ENVIRONMENT

NATIONS AND POLITICS

POEMS HERE AND THERE

PREFACE

Thinking about writing a few Autobiographical Notes, I happened to pull off the bookshelf *Riders on the Earth*, by Archibald MacLeish. I found autobiographical information and a lead.

Macleish asks himself when his commitment to poetry began, and leads us through an imagined conversation in which he answers an undergraduate's numerous questions about *becoming* a writer.

"*Becoming* a writer?" Macleish writes that Hemmingway left journalism because he *was* a writer. Macleish left a high-paying career in law, and took his family to Paris because of a persistent feeling that he owed something to Art.

By early college days I knew that I could write, was writing, but mostly occasional writings: for the college literary magazine an account of a solo boat trip down the Liard River, Northwest Territories; a dramatic piece for Parents Day at Wheaton College; the leading essay for a "Festschrift" celebrating C. S. Lewis; lots of etceteras, and some poems.

But then, taking a literature course at Drew University, I studied Wordsworth, John Donne, George Herbert, and other poets. Oh, I thought, this is poetry.

And then, late 60s, the English Department where I was teaching gathered on a weekend for one of those 60s events designed to give feelings some rein, in my case from the religious constraints with which I was raised.

I returned home and within hours wrote "Name;" and in the months and years that have followed a raft of poems, more than a few owing their existence to feelings given rein that weekend.

• • •

The poems you will read here come from the centuries-old character of poetry, poetry made from talk, the language of community.

ACKNOWLEDGEMENTS

My first attempt at publishing: I sent "First Born Prodigal" to Marcia Lee Masters (daughter of poet Edgar Lee Masters), editor of a Today's Poets column in the Chicago Tribune. She accepted. I said to Mack Stahl, a friend and fellow college teacher, "I'm published to millions." He said, "Here's how it goes: You read a poem to Martie, she says, 'I like it'—that's it."

A list follows: friends, who have liked poems I've shared, and encouraged the writing of poems.

Mack Stahl; Diane Anderson, former student; Diane and Dick Rosewall—Diane, who "devoured" new sends and Dick, who said early on, "Forget your textbook! Write (and publish) poetry; that's an order;" Sally Chappell Kitt and Walter Kitt, who gave loads of encouragement with insightful edits; Gladys Elliot, who kept the poems on her bedside table; Pete Jacobs; Martie Oury, for encouragement and edits of early poems; David Lindberg, Professor, University of Wisconsin, who treasured early poems; Clyde Kilby, professor of literature at Wheaton College, who launched me seriously into writing.

Recently, I have posted a poem a week to "Friends" on Facebook. Some have been actual friends and relatives; others, Facebook friends, the list growing by the week. From both categories I have received "Likes," and some short notes, personal and genuine (a hoped-for, but unexpected, pleasant surprise).

FLESH AND BLOOD

Song for My Beginnings

Geneva Community Hospital.
They have lost my birth certificate
and the sign says, "This Door Is Closed."
But I know it was here

in this steep-roofed, limestone mansion
shot with granite boulders
and slashed with a giant, tubular fire escape;
here behind the three, pointed gables
and windows offering row
on row of potted plants—I began.

Down the fire escape
she shot me into the middle of June.

They bundled me off over the green lawn
under the Burr Oaks and birdsong,
and over the river east in a
two-tone, tan Chevrolet.

There were just three of us then,
three for summer and sun,
two for prairie paths on Sunday mornings,
and one, mother says, walking first
with his hands reaching high for hold,
as if he reached for stars.

Mother of Eight

"You her favorite?—
she told you?"

Each child in us, unguarded,
opens a disbelieving face.

We are shocked only a moment.
We joke,
but each sends inarticulate questions
into that fragile world
where mother brooded
over only one.

Green Thumbs

Surprised?
As we two sit at breakfast
one day before mother's day—yes
surprised that your "variegated...
variegated (something) plants"
climbing along railroad ties towards each other
from opposite sides of the room
(these nameless with heart-shaped leaves)
have "turned up their noses with a sneer"
and slipped back home.

Without a slip of comprehension
you recite this litany
to each of us as we visit—surprised,
but delighted, too, in their mutual dislike;
"They know what they're doing," you say.

Down the timbered room, two by two,
I see you've trained them all,
all your philodendron the same—

Bless us.
Bless us all in search
of "the ties that bind."

"Lyric Pieces" (for Mother)

"I'll see you in heaven,
if not before," you said,
after perhaps the last kiss.
But heaven was
every time you touched the keys,
every time you trumped
the gilded morning with melody,
or trounced the storm
with the rolling thunder
of "The Ninety and Nine,"
or played—at ninety—nonstop
for an hour and more
in triumph at the old folks home
you left two years before.

Heaven—even when you could not hold
your head above the keys,
and strained to catch the fleeting melody—
the lyric touch, the touch, the touch

I sit listening to Grieg's "Lyric Pieces,"
tears welling and falling—you
should be playing them,
and we should be weeping together
for the first time.

Two Poems for Father

Ah, Father,
in this home you, dying, never knew,
mother's home,
young Bruce has walked into the room, quietly,
turned on another light,
and sat down to read.
I sit reading and listening to Brahms.
Father, father,
why has my heart suddenly broken again?

Presence—Father

Mornings at breakfast, sunroom,
I listen to symphonies in your presence.

Though absent six decades
you might as well be here, conducting,
as you did back then, those LP's:
The Sorcerer's Apprentice, Pier Gynt,
The Moonlight Sonata, and more,
introducing us kids to the classics.

This morning I'm tapping the rhythm of a symphony,
the quiet lyric of your company
permeating the morning air
over the silent stream of time.

First Born Prodigal

Father,
today,
unerringly,
I found my way
to your grave,
though the road branches and curves
and your plaque lies grass flat.

Three crows, raucous,
scattered to high branches
across the white stone road,
and I in dark dreams,
fear ridden,
dig down toward your mystery.

Prodigal, estranged,
searching,
returning so late
to a coffin,
a father's kiss exchanged
for crow's caws.

Eldest, wandering,
starved,
while the younger,
Fostered,
invested with inheritance,
feasted.

PSYCHE

On the Death of Ralph Hatcher
(general practitioner, neurologist, psychiatrist)

Last night one of those salty counselors,
lying by his wife, gave a start,
then died, controlled and quiet;
who would not suffer his patients the months of his fear,
nor to his strained heart give slack
in face of their constraint;
who counted the cost,
marked the sum,
and put his hand to the plow.

Last night an eagle fell
swiftly through blackness to cold ground.
Who heard his fledglings?
Who caught the confused cry
that disturbed the woods?
Whose eye searches,
whose wings cover
his covey of wounded creatures?
Who will mend them,
who with his lightning tenderness
will tend their stumbling flights?

Last night an eagle fell;
who searched the unyielding sky,
but spent his love upon these stricken creatures.

Greystone Park State Mental Hospital

For years you hung, a millstone on my mind,
threatening terminal of the damned.

But I had seen you only from a distance
and in my mind.

Today the bus pulls up and stops
by your grey bastions.
The unforgiven amble out.
Then we labor up, through,
and above you,
our doors clattering with the strain;
but not before you pose us a picture,
straggling, single file,
one of your damned little communities.
In the soft, autumn sunlight, Greystone,
you hang again on my mind.

"Miney"

All he has left are the threads
of his first, blue blanket.
It is his "miney."

From his mother's breast
he has dragged it all through his motherless world,
slept curled with it in his room,
gripped it tight against his cheek
in the empty afternoons.

Observe him now, years distant,
from a hidden corner of your mind.
The threads drift from his loosened fingers.
The door is ajar.
Through the narrow frame
he looks out upon the rich world, and opens.

Dream at Forty

Threatening primitives—ghastly corpses,
you came to my cave for the last time,
your weapons ineffectual.

The sweetening air—
I should have warned you—
your poison.

You lie contorted and bloodless;
I was ready for blows.

Grotesques,
ashen and stiff I spade you off
and into the butcher's trough.

Therapist (for Donna Ipema)

For a long time now she's been saying
that she loves me,
but so artfully
I heard only whispers caught glances
I did not believe.

Believed she might be attracted;
why these hugs, compliments
on my "command of the language,"
murmurs as I read poem after poem?

For a long time now you've been saying—
I didn't expect to leave week after week
with another rock laid into the foundation,
another strip of silver backing the mirror.

I expected trips to the cellar,
cobwebs and black widows,
beams rotting from seepage,
sewer pipes backed up.

Expected to be stung,
to replace timbers
with the weight of the house on my back,
to scoop crap.

But you've been telling me that you love me
and that the basement will hold.
Not telling, rather shining these—
They are not so much words . . .

It must be some art anonymous
(as Kierkegaard said it should be),
practiced at the margin of the mist-shrouded marsh
where you meditate,
or upon the dark side of the moon,
which underscores your luminous eyes.

Yes luminous.
All along you've been loving the only me that matters
with this luminescence.

FAMILY

Short Tribute—to Martie

You are music,
quiet melodies
played counterpoint
to the brass of your boys
and my double-belled euphonium.

Healing melodies,
Mending us.

Works of Love—for Martie
(remembering Kierkegaard)

So anonymous your love is,
unaware how it goes
or where,
my thirsting heart
finds the spring full,
silent, unnoticed.

Separation—to Martie

Bear with me a while,
for I miss you,
though I cannot say it well,
caught in conflicting passions
of which you are only a part,
coals dying in ash heaps,
flaming, playthings of the wind.

Be with me a while
apart, having loved bitterly,
out of my season.

Spring comes,
winter is passing.

Leave Taking Sans Sorrow
(upon his wife's departures for distant studies)

Of the family, the dog alone
faulted the virtue of your leaving,
slinking from the house tail down for the car.

We split the sleeping
morning with laughter,
threatened the bitch into staying,
and noised your going to the neighborhood.

But the town had been disquieted for days—
"a legalized affair—what sort of marriage?"

Nine years you
compassed my drift
and graced my circuits
with fair winds homeward,
a dove for the masthead.

Let me half so grace
your excellent goings and returns.

We will search new spheres,
and make an end worlds distant
from dead center.

Following Talk

Before the courtroom hearing,
we sat drinking coffee across the street.
The waitress, bantering with everyone,
brought the last pecan roll
and split it between us. "Share and
share alike," she said.

Later, out of our quiet, occasional talk,
you said, "The most poignant part of the Settlement
was about the boys, the words 'None were adopted.'"

Someone said you should send out
a birth announcement this spring—
am I bitter? The birthing was true,
I tell you, for both of us.

Now let the tears stream down
as they do in the old songs of separation.

I had not meant to talk to anyone for years.
Read the Judgment for yourself;
the boys were ours; look, our signatures.

Let's not talk anymore. Listen,
The final measures of Tchaikovsky's "Pathetique."

The Divorce

Tuesday—was it just Tuesday?

The cats doze it off,
one under the coffee table,
one on the couch.

The house is empty, furniture mute, radio off.
The refrigerator whirrs quietly.
Cars whisper back and forth on the street.
Overhead the muffled roar of a jet flying east.

I imagine calling someone,
"let's go somewhere,
talk, hold each other."

Departure (for Martie)

This three-masted schooner casts loose
from grey moorings and stands off in deeper water.
The rising sun washes bleached sails
aloft against blue sky.

A breeze approaching from the ocean
darkens a cloud patch of water near her.
She backs away from her eddies.
Her mainsails whip like giant, chained flags.
She falls off from the wind and lists.
Sharp reports crack off her sails.
Her keel digs a furrow against the weight of wind
as she begins to plow.

Garden

Evening, Ravel,
windows wide upon intoxicant spring,
leaf burst, pastels and purple sky.
Deep from a morning dream,
loneliness, amid friends and lovers—

would it have been different
if we had kept the garden?
If this evening we might have said, "dear."
Heard David call home from college,
John arrive home from hockey?

Garden we might have kept—
but out of which we birthed ourselves each.

Earlier today under your own sun
perhaps you walked the shore of Lake Zurich
in love or lonely.

I call you tonight and say,
How's the thesis coming?"
You laugh and say, "I'm writing songs."
We talk for an hour.

Who strikes, who is enemy
now that we have left paradise?

John Concentrated

He is stripping the black, plastic coating
off a silver, telephone cable.
His upper lip is pulled down white
inside his compressed, red, lower lip,
which pulls down his nose tip.

Breaths come in short puffs
released in rhythm
with the clip and tear of the plastic.

His head is bent to his work.
A tangle of blonde hair hides his eyes.

Shootin' (for John)

Bullseye in the backyard,
old marble-eyed TV
backed by an assortment of boards.

He stands on the ice pad
he's nurtured for a month.
Skirslap—whack!
Skirslap—whack!
Skirslap—crack!
Peg board fractures and flies.
Slap—ring, cyclone fence chimes in.

Slapitaslapitawhackitaslapit—
neighboring garages racket reply
under Chicago's halogen skies and a half moon.
Neighborhood's listening.

To David at Twelve Years

I sit down to write, "My boy,"
but the words get stuck.

This is no kid.
The eyes shoot sparks—he says,
"Maybe for you,
not for me."
Bully is not beautiful.

The eyes hurt in quiet.

The eyes reflect a deep pool of thoughts,
speckled, brown, silver, rainbow,
a thousand thousand circling,
diving, drifting, flashing.
All are kept,
none are lost.

The eyes say,
I'm not quite like anyone else.
And I'm glad.

For David and John

It is late afternoon
And I am back from packing the wilderness
we made home for nine days,
you strapping sons,
your mother,
some friends,
and I.

I glance down and notice your child selves
in a photograph brandishing sticks at me.

What did you know then of offense,
you with those innocent sticks?
Against what harm, defenseless,
did you take up arms? I

have left you again;
is it only I
who have noticed?

The afternoon sun brightens my hanging fern,
hearth, and mantle—these tears,
do they well and spill only for you?

In every child alone
I picture the offense.

I weep, my sons, for myself,
the child alone and defenseless;
and for you,
though you are strapping and strong,
and hold me harmless.

For the Wedding, David and Jae

Colorado Sports Bar, Denver airport,
Vanessa Williams and Maria Sharapova
on TV playing a tennis match
we're watching with a hundred or so persons
we might have met; but we exchange just a word
with a friendly guy next table.
"She won this match yesterday," he says of Vanessa,
who's playing today only on TV.

How did you two meet?
Who first said, "hello?"
Who responded?
What chemistry kept the exchange from being brief,
the match from being played yesterday?

Marriage is the magic coincidence
you've sustained for years.
Over the years may it live
a long and happily coincident life.

Father John at Forty-Six

Steady, steady as he goes in storm and calm,
steady when the wind suddenly shifts and waves
drop and heave.
Steady when the leaden sky lowers
and the gale spits in his face.
Steady and still plowing with the sea rippling,
sun dancing on the water.

Steady with the child upset by desertion,
the mother who fled.
Steady with the child of the charged brain,
tirades one moment, friendly the next.

Steady at the helm of the giant ship
called marriage, a wife whose worries whip the surface,
while his plunge the deep and break surface.

Steady, steady, and
loving, father, John.

David at Forty-Seven

You are forty-seven, yet keeping still
a "deep pool of thoughts,
speckled, brown, silver, rainbow,
a thousand thousand" now ordered,
exponentially expanded from boyhood.

You are "not quite like anyone else,"
not that that concerns you now.
You play upon the elementary shapes of Category Theory,
discs and trees with definitions,
at first glance, down to earth.
"The coproduct of a collection of trees
is a forest" (well of course).
"A forest map, a natural transformation of forests,
pruned" (mapping and horticulture made easy).
Definitions all but homey—until you mix and match:
"Category Disc has objects called *discs*,
which are finite cropped labeled trees" (hmmm).
Then comes "Glob Card category equivalent[s],"
and homey is lost forever.

Yet you are at home, your laser-like thought concentrated
on shapes, relations and functions familiar,
to us strange as galaxies,
strange as quantum particles, here and there at once,
strange as string theory, dark matter.

But you're still our flesh and blood,
with the winsome voice and soul tender as a lamb;
our hunter too, taut as a bow, arrow strung,
set dead on for bull's-eye.

Nostalgia for Fall

If it were only again September, sun aslant,
smolder and lick of fire on leaf mound,
flame scattered upon branch and leaf.

As if it were September again,
to stand excited and noisy on the corner
waiting for the school bus.

Or to be off for college,
green lawns raked with sun,
the wide world in prospect.

Or to begin family again
in the little bare colonial by the woods,
under the young Shagbark Hickory,
stripping wallpaper, patching cracks, painting;
making terraces, planting the new lawn,
planting rhododendron, mountain laurel and dogwood,
but this time easy with love and children,
this time easy with talks and walks and trips.

It is September and always again September,
scent of leaf mold and smoke,
flame on mound and branch,
the old leavings organic
or burning in imagination.

I round the corner of my sidewalk
under the limb-torn chestnut
tipped with red,
the flickering of love.

CHRISTIANITY

Name

How shall we call upon Him
of whom we have heard?

"O thou, enthroned in glory,
we beseech thee,
ministerially,
hear thy people
gathered this morning
row upon upright row."

"O Lord of Hosts,
that this multitude claim thy name,
we aim;
that they grasp thy name en masse,
we ask;
that they say 'we do,'
nor rue our cue;
that they finish all fine,
sign on the line
for thy name's sake."

"We thank thee, dear Lord,
that thou hast blessed thine own
righteous remnant,
and prospered the works of our lips.
And we rejoice
that we are not
as other men,
that we are not"—
God!

Now that lechers have drawn the wine,
And leeches the blood,
since Cornelius rejects the Sunday visitation,
the Ethiopian Eunuch the message broadcast;
since the millstones are late
in drowning the voices that offend,
upon whom will they call?

Spirit where it will,
in the heart's core
storming and still,

what voice yet speaks
in the raging
and the winding?

Gathering Song
(performed at Northminster Church, Evanston, IL)

Oh God we gather
in peace and concord,
appearances pleasant and light.

Good morning, good Sunday,
good Lord, Sunday morning,
good morning we give thee this day.

Oh Christ we come
in chaos and discord,
with hearts that are troubled and dark.

Good morning, good Sunday,
good Lord, Sunday morning,
good morning we give thee this day.

Lord have mercy.

In our hearts in shadow,
beneath our bright show,
we are counting the profit and loss,
suffering the struggles of a distant son or daughter,
watching winter sift through our loves.

Christ have mercy.

Shadow partners walk the secret
passageways of our minds.
Glib disguises glaze our distraught faces.
The accusing judge sits heavily upon our hearts.

Oh Lord hear our prayer.

We would praise
And lift our song,
but our hearts wind the back ways
bruised and searching.

Lord have mercy.
Christ have mercy.
Oh Lord hear our prayer.
We offer our hearts this day.

Corelli, Adagio, Christmas

Golden, golden, adagio,
spun from your strings;
you gather, send upon us silence,
and richly tune our waking hearts.

Golden, golden, adagio,
spin finest gold;
gather, send among us peace,
and richly tune our waking hearts.

Minister and Wife

The minister this morning is urging,
exhorting us forthrightly to righteousness
with the upturned palm of his right hand.

His left arm is crooked behind his back,
the middle and ring fingers lightly pressing to his palm
the sleeve of his black robe.

Smiling and stiff offered her welcomer's hand.
Relaxed an instant as she turned away.
Put up a smile for the next, no one
was

The church is not between them today;
together in the second row
they take in the Christmas cantata.
She leans toward him with a nod elsewhere.
They smile.

He leans back, his arms spread wide upon the pew.
From the waist up he beats time to "Every valley. . ."
rolls his rollicking head and merry, red face.

She is a meadow,
a peaceful and attentive doe
far from public.
They lean toward each other conspiring.
The light growing upon them is unstained.

Men's Choir

The center isle is full of bulls;
the grace at the right hand is gone.

The processional unsprings
with heavy tread and rocking shoulders
as for stampede, jams to a stop,
unsprings again jams.
Then docile, proceeds to chorale.

They stand self-conscious, sheepish.
But deep down the bellows fill.

The Congregation at the Sermon

With open faces we wait,
attentive, expectant.
Ministering fingers drop shades before our eyes.
Calloused palms cradle our chins
and turn our faces aside.
We lift the shades,
face forward once more and wait,
attentive (God help us), expectant.

Sermon

Take life as it comes, he said,
who took less care for his than birds and foxes.
One day's trouble is enough for one day.
Surely life is more
than next month's cost of living,
than silverware and hors d'oeuvres,
than impending failure, fears of separation,
more than dread of dying.

One day's trouble is enough.
Surely life out of a day's dying,
surely beauty.
Consider the lilies.

Christian Commitment

"There is no better way to show our Christian commitment than to put our names and money on the line."

Are you uncertain?
We must continue;
we must keep things up!
Are you wondering? Listen!

Your money or your life!
You devil, sign.

Reformation Sunday

This is Reformation Sunday.
No more Papas!
No more distinction between minister
and laymen, Gospel we publish!
The fullness of the faith we trumpet.

Never
our transcendent diction
mind. Never
the ceremonial suppression of self awareness
mind.
We have the print out, your
pattern.

Christians and Others

These dear friends, salt of the earth,
and countless like-minded believers,
who follow the Savior, feed the hungry,
heal the sick and wounded,
visit the imprisoned—give away their lives,
having made home this way-station to a better world—
Bless them all.

Bless as well the agnostics and atheists,
indistinguishable from the believers,
who work for a world beyond.

Bless all who believe in a better world
and labor to give it birth.

Changing the World

Most of us would change the world,
of course to make it better.

Many would like to exchange the world
for another altogether.

But we're stuck on our own little patch of earth
in a universe vast and strange,
to turn the soil and plant our plot
and wait patiently for change.

Love your neighbor he said;
observe the effect
on the neighbor next to him.
Love your enemy, too;
observe the effect
on the enemy next to him.

We all would like to change the world
and I would change it too.
It could happen if I began with myself,
and you—perhaps with you.

Lovers of Children

"Let the little children come to me," Jesus said,
sat them on his lap and embraced them.

But he did not defile their laps,
invite them to the seaside,
take them to his retreats
or to his carpenter's shop in Nazareth.

If anybody should offend just one, Jesus said,
he should be drowned, roped by the neck to a millstone
to make sure.

At the current news imagine him coming
to the Temples whip in hand,
raising hell and calling on heaven
to rain down such destruction
as would make Sodom and Gomorrah
child's play.

Forgiveness

On his rampage perhaps he should have paused,
for a moment, this master of the Temple discussion,
master of the Word, to hear the Apologies.

Forgiven, we will go and sin no more at this place.

The victims waited too long.
The priest is dying; pardon a life of sin.

These reports are a campaign to discredit the Church.
We are being persecuted—like the Jews, like you!

Scandal is a sin in and of itself.
Molestation is a secular crime
(There are no crimes within the Church).

Finally, the Cardinal-now-Pope—is the Pope!
Self evidently beyond accusation. Case closed.

Meanwhile, from these living temples of the Spirit,
these defiled, the cries arise—and gather.

Nearness

The nearness of God is the nearness of persons.
Through the storm Jesus is brought to sight
and all is right.
Gide's nursemaid comes into view;
The dark valley is flooded with light [1]

Perhaps you were reading fiction.
From the page as if in the flesh
leapt a kindred soul;
at a moment's will,
with you still.

Presence is enough.
You've felt it in the valley's shadow,
a touch, a caress, an unexpected call
in the moment of despair,
as if the heavens cared,
as if a person coming near
was enough to banish fear,
erase despair—the nearness of persons
is the nearness of God.

[1] Vandenberg, The Changing Nature of Man

PERSONS

Marcia's Place (for Marcia Lee Masters)

She takes you in obliquely
looks at you aslant.
For an instant her eyes meet yours;
she heard what you were saying.

Her place is full of sun,
full of sun and the leaves
at the water's edge,
the translucent, green leaves
suffused with sun
that slow sunlight into the shadowed woods.

Her place is at the edge of the sea
where the waves break.
She listens.
The mists rise to her high balcony.

The winds rush her balcony
and blow her thoughts away;
she writes in the library.

She has a statue of Venus,
but it's off for sale.
In its place are prickly, spiny cacti.
Her cacti take in the sun
and feel in their roots the incessant break of waves.

Out of its spikes one
Offers a red blossom
For the waves and the sun.

Gladys Eliot
(principal oboist, Lyric Opera)

"God's instrument,"
was all she said.
I imagine the principals,
their instruments in cases,
coming to listen.

In concert I hear them say
what one said actually:
"*That* is enough inspiration
to last ten years."

Her eyes are bright and intent,
her head tilted slightly
as if she were teaching,
and she says,
"we are only his instruments."

Gladys—Commuters

The week before Christmas,
walking to her towers after opera rehearsal,
rush hour, a numbing Loop wind,
she stepped off the fractured curb
and flung herself, instrument and all,
upon the street.

"No bus ran me over," she said;
"I was glad for that."
A Black man pulled her over
to sit on the curb past which
commuters rushed for trains.
"I'm a little stunned, but O.K.," she said.
He left.
"Taxi," she cried
for ten minutes;
she could not rise on her fractured foot.

"Taxi," she cried,
for twenty minutes more,
while they rushed by to trains.
"I was dressed well,
And my bags were of good quality," she said.

Then the cold got to her;
she began to tremble.
And of a passerby politely
demanded relief from her condition.

For Gladys, Comatose

You sleep.
Brute circumstance has bludgeoned you again
beyond all proportion,
the blind city bus bashing you into the curb,
the orb of sight into the heaven of your understanding.

You sleep.
While your mind remakes itself
we mark the days with weeping,
our supplications streaming to you—
would that weeping might make your mind whole,
mend the broken body.

You sleep.
In bleak dreams far from shore,
far from the Thanksgiving home on the point,
again you walk the edge of ice.

You sleep.
Cradle life as you walk the margin,
life for all of us.

For Dick Rosewall

(following the news of cancer, late October)

Clouds in grey flannel stride across the blue sky
as if heaven is theirs alone,
yet leaving pools of blue, rimmed with gold.
Beyond the field of dusky goldenrod
the tightly wrapped buds of birches burn dull red
hoarding coals for the distant flame of spring.

The mild, mellow days of Indian summer
flee winds from the Pole,
snow in the Dakotas, gales in Chicago,
frost heavy on field and barn
just below the patch of earth on which we dwell.

Beyond field and wetland, rank on rank
of leaf-stripped ash, oak, maple,
and golden birch hold their ground
while season slides to season.

Richard

Richard is gone,
who will never again sit,
St. Bernard, seal, walrus,
watching with hardly a turn of head
or flick of observant eyes.

Who will no longer listen
without so much as a twitch
to our talk far into the night.
Who will not reach down to touch
either Dachshund
or draw them up
to his lap
for snuggles.

Richard is dead,
who will not again
by the barred, grime stained windows
sit tasting, who never again
will taste the richness
still our lease.

Aunt Alice

You weigh only about a hundred now,
perhaps less without that mess of a leg
they took off above the knee a week or so ago.

But your voice is still as resonant
and smooth as a cello—
singer, uncle Wall said
still sent chills down his spine.

Your face is that of a queen,
sharp featured and noble, graced
with sweeps of hair steel grey.
I watch waves of pain wash your face.

"They won't give me my hit," you say—
"What are they doing now?
Tell me about your brothers.
Tell me about your boys."

You respond to my report
with evaluations perceptive and precise;
you have kept perfect track all these years.

"Do you have lady friends?" you ask.
You do not accept my deferential reply; you say,
"I'll bet you have lots of lady friends."

I bend to the wheelchair
which you have made a seat of state
and kiss you on the lips as I leave.

Janet and Bob Ross

She was slight of stature, but a
"stubborn old coot," he said,
"hard as nails, tough—
you met her.
Fantastic sense of design;
you'll see when you come to the house.

"Did everything her way;
did what she wanted to do,
design houses, create businesses,
travel wherever she fancied,
all the continents but Antarctica—
sent her husband there instead."

Bob, who was by her side every step,
by her side, a teetotaler by choice,
so that she wouldn't miss a step.

Miss a step—did I mention
that she had brain cancer all those years,
that she was given three years to live,
that she and that husband at her side
said no, not yet, joined battle,
and fought death to a standstill—
for thirty-five long, glorious years.

One in a million, fought death
to a standstill and carved out
for themselves, Life.

Sandra
(for Sandra Williams)

This is real,
but she is more
real than this.
More real than the cancers
multiplying residence
in her breasts and lungs, and brain.

She will not have that;
she will have her indomitable spirit,
only that, as Real.

And those unwelcome residents—
let them stay and die.
She, as Auden said of Yeats,
will become her admirers,
will take up residence in us.

The Love of Living

All is as it should be with old friends,
Stan and I in the kitchen, Stan chatting away
as he fixes a fancy eggplant parmigiana—
"Got it at North Park Produce, Mid-Eastern.
The people there are extraordinarily friendly."

Our wives are conversing in the living room,
soft voices. The evening has cooled.
Sandra calls out to check a fact
in the last Doc Martin episode.
"I told Sandra," Stan says, "that the farmer's wife
had died."

Let me say that Sandra is expected
shortly to—but will not—die,
if she has anything to do with it.
So far, for sure, she has.

So. Mix with this oh-so-human
evening's chatter a good pinch of
salt of the earth, vinegar, adamant, guts,
and whatever else is needed
in the fading light to extend even a little,
or longer, the love of living.

Sandra—Burial at Sea

The rest burned away,
we take to sea what remains of her,
when poured off the stern to a calm ocean
incandesces to a cloud of florescent aqua,
over the grey depth holding shape as we circle,
luminescent.
Like her.

Women in Transition

(for the WITS writing class)

The subject was pain.
The object, potential.
The verb was laughter
facing disaster.

Roses are red,
violence is you;
will violet ever
be mated to blue?

Dad beat me early,
dad beat me late;
dad beat me whenever
he deemed it my fate.
But I've penned my outrage;
I've written my wit,
stronger by far
than the almighty whip.

Papa's got drunk
and will wreck the homestead;
but I've got the bullet
he'd put in his head.

Dad taught me early
my lessons in sex;
but I've learned far more
than he'd ever have guessed.
Dad taught me early,

no pleasure in that;
but pleasure's my bedfellow,
now that's a fact.
I'm beautiful, I'm sexy,
I've got pain in my bowels;
I'm fierce, I'm Black,
I'm the lady who growls.

I'm Latin, I'm lovely,
I live in the barrios;
don't mess with me mister,
my talents are various.

I'm the woman who's white;
my dad warned me of college.
But now is my hour;
I turn doomsday to knowledge.

I'm the iconoclast, image breaker,
form smashing woman,
up in the middle of the night
to write the pain away.
(I'll spare you my choice words.)

I'm the woman whose dad stole fifteen years,
who's husband almost stole the rest.
I'm the woman getting them back,
the woman who walks in the park,
feeds the ducks, smells the roses,
picks them and takes them home for my own.

I'm the street girl from the Bronx
who never heard of slavery,
the one listening to her mind break free.
Is that me?

I'm the crazy guy here,
swimming through his own sea of troubles,
all seven seas if you like clichés.
I don't have time for clichés;
Big Y takes all my time.

I'm the Black man here.
I write rap, poetic rap.
Just yesterday Lamont and I got pulled over—
driving while Black.
Spent twenty minutes in the rain
while the trooper emptied our car.
Women, I hear you.

I'm the mother whose mother left her,
a child alone in the violent house.
I'm the child who wrote the violence
all over her mattress through the long night,
then left to join her mother,
leaving a message too large to ignore.

We are women in transition
taking a long trip,
going far,
on the boat together,
on the Orient Express,
flying United.

Someone special has been waiting patiently for us
at the port, the depot, the gate.
When we arrive she will say,
with a smile as wide as the miles,
"My darlings, welcome."

FRIENDS AND LOVERS

Witchery

Tonight the house and nearby trees
are haunted by women.
None of their shades are white;
with veils burning bright cherry,
burgundy and wine,
this witchery, they drift in.
And over the lightly fallen snow
I feel my cool bedroom flame.

Allenspark Autumn, Willow Creek

Leaves of aspen white and yellow,
flat as lily pads on little pools.

Broken trunk and branch
soaking in rivulets.

Firebrick flame scattered in barberry
up the ski run slash in the pines.

Yellow aspen, sun-suffused,
crisp, pointillist,
adrift down the canyon.

Season by season
scatterings of desire
over the rivulets of time,
and still pools
reflecting an evening sky.

Robin

And then a Robin,
through the open front window alight
on a rail
in the morning
sun, earth
orange and grey, who
curved her neck, looking
back from where she'd flown,
as if to say, contrary
to appearances, I'm
somewhere else.

Hawkeyed Beauty

You're taller tonight
in spite of your wide-striped turtleneck,
you there, hawkeyed brunette,
sitting across from me at a distance
so collapsed we could be kissing.

We're talking,
jazz, counterpoint, folk
themes incipient of symphony,
hour on hour the sort of music we're used to,
just talking,
not kissing.

Sharing Something

It was not so much the wine colored dress
so lightly lying on your shoulders and hips,
and billowing bell-shaped at your elbows;

nor the fine curtain-fall of blonde hair
staging your face
alive with a quick and curious intelligence.

More the sense of a brief engagement,
my own heart tendered to dreams the night before,
yours uncurtained for a moment
with thoughts of love to lose.

More just us,
strangers without a claim,
talking.
It was only a little talk
I found myself remembering
next to tears.

Mirror

I am your mirror.

This shameless embrace,
the shape of your own liking.

These eyes,
your flashing.

This clown
returns your wrinkling smile.

Yet something of myself alone
returns to you grateful tears
you have never yet shed.

For Her Beauty

If I had not heard your voice,
voice the color of your flaming red hair;
or seen you lean so sinuously into the melody,
I would have taken you for a painting by Botticelli.

Ficus

I am a tall, broad
leaf, Ficus Elastica.
I stretch red tips toward the sun,
unfolding leaf after leaf.
The flood ripples over my green skin.
I toe deep into black earth and root.
And say to the earth from which I rise,
"How have you grown a plant so beautiful?"

Owning the Light

Your face appears now
as I watched it catch the light
slanting from bay windows
and change the evening light
filtered down from the Ficus,
catch and change the light
as if you owned it.

Your face appears.
I watch until you draw home
all that is left of daylight,
and gather in the dusk.

Purple Heart

Perhaps they had blossomed
before you came;
but not until Sunday
did I notice tiny violets
spring bell-like from leaf axils.

Some have shriveled since you left;
but some point tiny new spears
for your return.

Poem in Love (to my father)

It is a warm, sunny afternoon
in the late summer, father,
and I am in love

with a woman of such beauty and grace
as once, for a while, you knew.

Again I find your final place,
with an exactness I wouldn't have guessed,
brush the mown grass
from the bronze face you now present,
stand, and catch a glint of sun
from the spare letters
that spell out your span.

Father,
foster the gentle and loving self
you must have known;
let love as fine as you once knew
grow with me.

The Turning

This morning I listened
to Handel's oboes filling my living room
with their exquisite counterpoint.

I went in and stood in the center,
entranced and reflective;

then turned and saw the fern,
the arch and fall of its branches
suffused in a slant of sun.
And then the tears began.

I turned and remembered its misting,
and went, you may understand, weeping
for water to make a fine mist.

And weeping hard, turned
and turned it to the spray,
watching the little mists
sift in the sunlight through its shoots,
and settle upon its thickening skirts.

Buckeye—Break Up

You can hardly see it tonight,
just that street lamp, bold and blank,
glaring in at the window
past where great arms and shoulders
shrugged off the sky,
and curtains of five-foliate fingers
shrouded that simple, staring eye.

In April you could have seen
its two huge boles, and branches in leaf
lofting over rooftops against the sky,
but for one great, topmost branch
torn off and stretched upon the lawn,
its blossoms, fresh with rain,
strewn upon the grass.

Late in May you saw
what was left of those loftings
face a towering twist of sky
that gathered its greatness from the horizons;

heard the oaks and elms
a block on either side
uproot, crack and splinter;

shuddered as a giant bole
was wrenched from the trunk,
and shook with the house
as its great branches fell upon the gables,
rolled, and grazing its windows,

cracked and shattered along half the length
of its foundations.

A tree stands now by half
spreading arms for its familiars:
squirrels who leap and play
upon bowed bridges solid as stone;
Sparrows and Wrens who have forgotten
lofty perches firm as rock;
and a great, ungainly Raven
who walks upon the topmost branch,
blinking at the splintered trunk.

A tree by half now stands.
Tonight its back is turned
upon the street lamp's glare.

No Respect

Have you no respect for this sullen earth?
Will you have the whole world
break into song?

This harsh, March wind
scouring the last snows
brushes my dwelling,
but with a soft note,
like your voice.

Lowering clouds
break and lace with sun,
like your smile.

Even mechanical devices are touched.
Radios around me this morning
erupt with symphony.
This evening my little brown diesel,
cruising along the swollen river,
drops its muffler, clears its throat,
and hums like a Cossack chorus Ah,

I am humming too, Love,
let it break into song;
let's find an instrument to play it right,
take lessons; this music is too much
for either one of us unskilled, or alone.

Dancer

The thought of you, dancer,
light as lift
then drifting down
as if to dissipate in air.
Three shivers shake my spine;
tears, burning like salt,
well and spill like sea.

I lie full length
and let the sea, oh dancer,
dancer, come with me.

Overture

Come.
This is an old invitation,
an overture with eighteen cannon
and cathedral bells from twelve steeples.

Come.
The orchestra sits expectant.
Across the grass hills of Grant Park
the giants rise silent within the muted Loop.

Look!
the skyscrapers conspire with the rising sun,
and one by one burst with fire.

Come.
The symphony has begun.

Note

Inside a folded note
you may find
more than a poem.
With your touch
I unfold,
fold me
in folds, I
am flesh
and feeling.

Venus Rising

I gave my love to the Botticelli I saw.
She was not what I imagined.

She rose in a flashing so fast
I could not fix her coming.

Demure?
Her hands were vices.

Gentle breezes, placid landfall?
Breakers on rock falls, gulls' cries.

For all the surprise,
Venus still, rising,
that soft, unbraiding rope of hair,
and unmistakably the eyes.

Planetarium

Copper, copper,
on a pleasure cruise, quite—
don't interrupt—
us, cruise on by.

You cannot police the fog
horn soft as doe,
nor ticket the wind
rustling elm leaves above,
nor summon the mist
silent as stolen time
drifting from sea
to shroud our spread of stars.

My love and I
are the horn and the sea,
the wind that wakes the tree,
the mist, the sky.
Cruise on by.

Clock at 3:00

I have no tongue
for the picture of you
lying with me
like the hands of a clock at three.

I have the picture's gloss,
its luster in your luminous eyes,
when for a moment or two
you drew the veils.

Venus Disguised

You wear so well your disguises
it was hours after we had scattered them
upon the table, dresser and floor
that I noticed,

though all night you held me
in that wistful gaze,
asking only realization.

I woke with recognition:
"Venus," I said.
"Yes," you answered,
with no more exposition
than a goddess might give.

Love

Love
like sun emblazoned Aspen
against spears of pine
on the near ridge;

like Aspen in dabs and brush strokes,
yellow and orange on the far ridge
under massive rock outcroppings,
among the pine green and grey.

A watercolor sky, pastel blue,
over soft, grey clouds.

The late morning air,
still.

Exposé

Half the night you make me sit with you
under the glare of halogen lights
in the center of the park.

As we walk over the rush hour expressway
without warning you turn to embrace,
witnessed in the crisp morning air
by dozens of eyes uplifted.

Against your public principles
you turn wherever you please,
touch, kiss, embrace,
say silly things,
sing zip i dee doo dah—
if they could only hear.

I'm crazy myself, publicly,
around, about, with, over you,
without a thought as to how pleased
anyone else is
but us.

Great Expectations

"I can feel the cold winter coming,"
you said, "and it's sad."

Yes, I thought,
the sadness wise bliss expects;
let's speak it and make it scarce,
who never spoke nor expected love
like this.

Making Love I

You lie beneath my strain, crush and kiss,
compassed by my tensed embraces.

I am in flight,
a single shaft—bull's eye
in the making scarcely feeling
your caresses—you intercept;
"Let me kiss you," you say.

You sit astride
sensing my impulse to rise and encircle.
In the instant I feel your palms
flat upon my forearms, and you begin.

Upon dawn scarcely lighter than the elm leaves
I hear the sparrow's song.

Making Love II

Her touch, slim fingers
curl over my hip bone, cup,
"come here."

"Kiss me," I say,
"kiss me."

"That's—
'damn it,
kiss me'—
personal,
nothing personal."

Making

There's a special joy in making,
whatever the thing may be;
a special joy in making babies,
though the product takes months to see.

And a lasting pleasure in making love,
when there's nothing left in sight,
but the pleasure of love
making love through the night.

Wild Caves

Entering them is,
however thrilling, not it.
The passage ends.
Those little siphon holes corkscrewing
down from the final chamber
do not lead anywhere,
only drain the flood.

But you think: virgin cave—
it's mine alone.
You twist back out of the narrow passage;
it slows your retreat, presses from all sides.

Other wild caves will
end you the same,
turn you back where you came;
but noticing, perhaps,
discarded flashlight batteries,
grey scars of used carbide on the wall;
and thinking that passages
are shared alike.

The surge of feeling that goes
with the passage into virgin territory lasts
a little longer,
and is also isomorphic.

But the landscape, experienced inside out, is not.

The next curve of the unending passage
branching into mysteries,
intricate box work extruding from ceiling cracks,
ivory flowstone lucent in still, looking glass pools, stalactite and stalagmite caught,
God and Adam arms outstretched,
in the act of creation.

And a bowl branched by pine and fir,
its clear pond seeping, like love,
into the loosening interstices of limestone,
feeding springs flowing pure and cold
from the roots of the hills.

Opposites

Since the fire within
sometimes glows like coals;
and sometimes crackles with a crisp German accent;

Since you can slave like any farmer
in overall drab
and wrap rainbow, light on light
to your contours;

and since you lie open like a meadow
and hidden like a cave,
would at once love
and leave,

I come warm as sun on the bedspread,
intimate as the envelope of body heat
under morning covers,
and burn star point
in the vast chastity of space.

Time Together

Last night you played Mimi,
while I sat writing the words you were saying
all excited—"look at this sash;
it's so beautiful, the craft,
the textures I love to feel—
did I tell you, shall I be a designer?"

More Musetta
you donned and doffed designs,
gowns and dresses.

Then we conversed our love
and our constraint,
late and in our fashion,
but with such clarity
little was left
to say.

So I stood to go,
we embraced,
locking for an instant
lightly head to toe.

Then from your lips just kissed
escaped the sigh.

Nothing more tangible than a sigh
leaves me this morning in a peace so sensual I—
a thousand miles severed, less sensible we
live some inscrutable lie.

The Afternoon—Fragments

On this afternoon
slowly graying the white snow
that fell fresh and weightless just yesterday,
under a perfectly gray and featureless sky,
I remember the "bright yellow day."

The grassed and tan folds of hills
across the small valley of mesquite.
We walked down through dry grass
and along the dusty road,
light with interplay of hands and hugs,
dancing our distance, we walked.

No place to sit or lie;
sun-curled chips of clay dry
as crackers curled up brittle edges.
Barbed wire fenced off the river.
We spread a blue jacket
and a shirt the color of clay.

Fine straggles of black branches
on the crystal air in the stillness.

You ducked my kisses.
"I feel so shy with you," you said.

A cool and distant sun,
glazing brushes of clouds far west.

I stood, the broken stems
of weeds in my hair.
"Leave them there," you said.

White Brahmans up from the river
ran noiselessly along the fence,
dust rising under and behind them.

You found the lock washer,
the broken ring.
You found the washer with the tight center,
and the screw.

The freeway was dark at our return.
Halfway twin buttes loomed high to the left.
"The magical mountains," you said.
You were kissing my index finger then.
I stopped to draw you in.
You ducked my kiss again,
but lay your head upon my thigh.
I held you there,
and through the darkness drove.

Keeping House

Take care, friend, lest you slip,
and fall to lover—beware.
Behind the grass skirt I keep
a broom made of sterner stuff,
and sweep my place clean.

Don’t Talk

Don’t
talk to me; don’t
talk to me of

kindness, feel
this lily’s razor edges; don’t
talk to me of

passions, the effusive blossoming
of this tulip tree, observe
its branches hybrid of hawthorns; don’t
talk to me of

love, come longing
to this luminous rose
hidden deep in a thicket of briars;
don’t talk to me.

Planting

I have planted a garden,
hoed and trenched until I trembled,
then watered in the late afternoon
with a child's bucket.

I water evening times
waiting for seed to burst and root
in this silent earth.

April

I wait for you
watching the early signs of spring
under a winter's sky and rough winds.

Through my window I see
the fingered leaves of buckeye blossom,
starlings from grey branches
dive to the green lawn, strut and peck.
A nimble squirrel outlines an arching branch,
then in a hump feeds upon the blossoming
heart of a bud.

Come,
bring the full blossoming
and heart of spring.

For the Last Day of Summer

I went to gather a poem, love,
for the last day of summer,
but the day was still green,
apples bough by bough
tinged with green,
green longings.

Today the burdened apple tree
lifts and shakes its crimson head
fresh with the first gusts of fall.

Listen!
Raining staccato
upon grasses and sod,

taste again,
take to your soil.

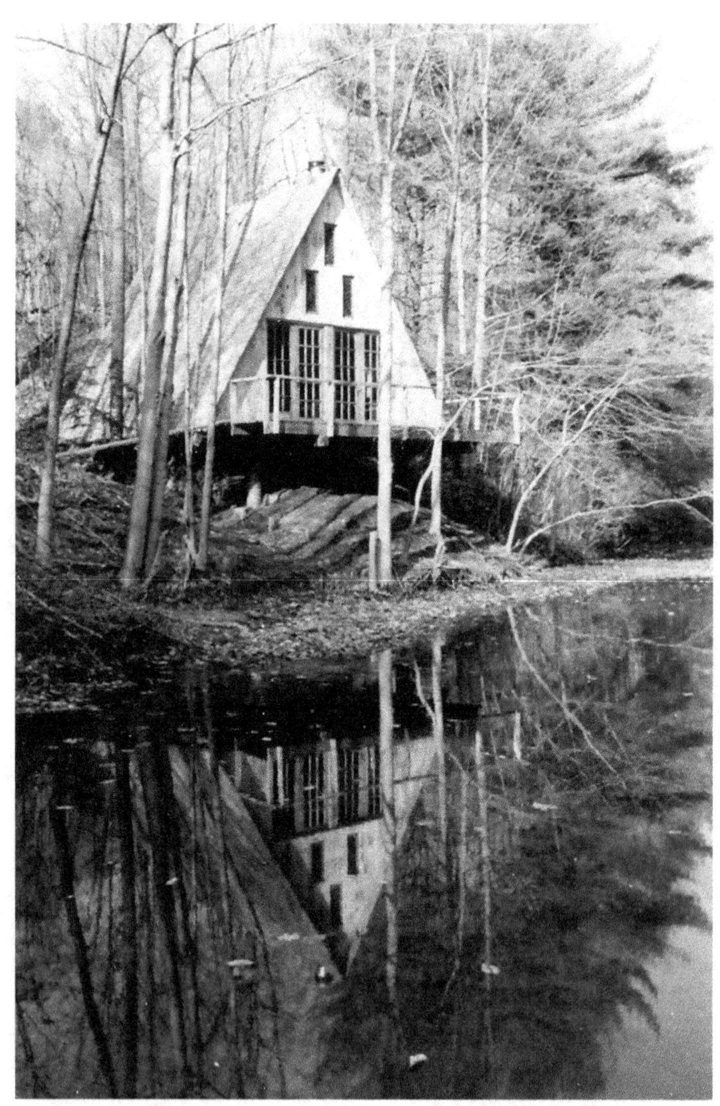

New Moon by Half
(at the A-frame)

Only an oboe,
plaintive tonight upon loneliness
as old as mind.

An oboe under the stillness of bare maples,
a half moon rising,
stars pointing the sky.

Then an owl out on the ridge hooting twice;
and across the wooded valley an answer.

My intimate my stranger, minding stars
I make a place for us on this little patch of earth.

Lying alone in this stillness older than mind
I fashion a dwelling intimate
as this cabin in the woods, and spacious
as a heaven of stars.

For Life

Life is not what you hoped,
because you hoped it would be—pleasant,
the occasional wound superficial,
a cut on the forearm.

Life is the cut to the quick.
Your Irish Setter found dead in the roadside ditch,
the piano sonata from the radio as you drive off.

Your wife, the night you said she could leave,
in a dream, dancing.

The flutist styling upon your heart
the departure of your Platonic lover.

Life is not the occasional sickness,
chicken pox or four days of scarlet fever,
but knowing the disease deep and persistent
as your very own,

knowing that both your anger and concern were misplaced,
that the fearful diagnosis is incomplete,
that the doctor will not come at midnight,
that you must practice cures.

Life is not the middle of the storm—crisis,
your automatic reactions,
but in the dead silence, lightning.

And again lightning, invited this time
to the full-length mirror in your family closet,
the slivers of glass in hand after the shattering,
the labor to piece and pattern.
Life, having given away love,
life is giving up your current passion,
lying alone at the edge of the bed,
your heart breaking,
yet knowing, once that is done,
peace rising still and certain as dawn
upon your unwilling acceptance.

Life is knowing, finally,
that no one will come to save,
knowing as if it were Scripture
that you must work out your own salvation
in fear and trembling.

Yet knowing,
in the valley of the shadow of death,
a certain grace.

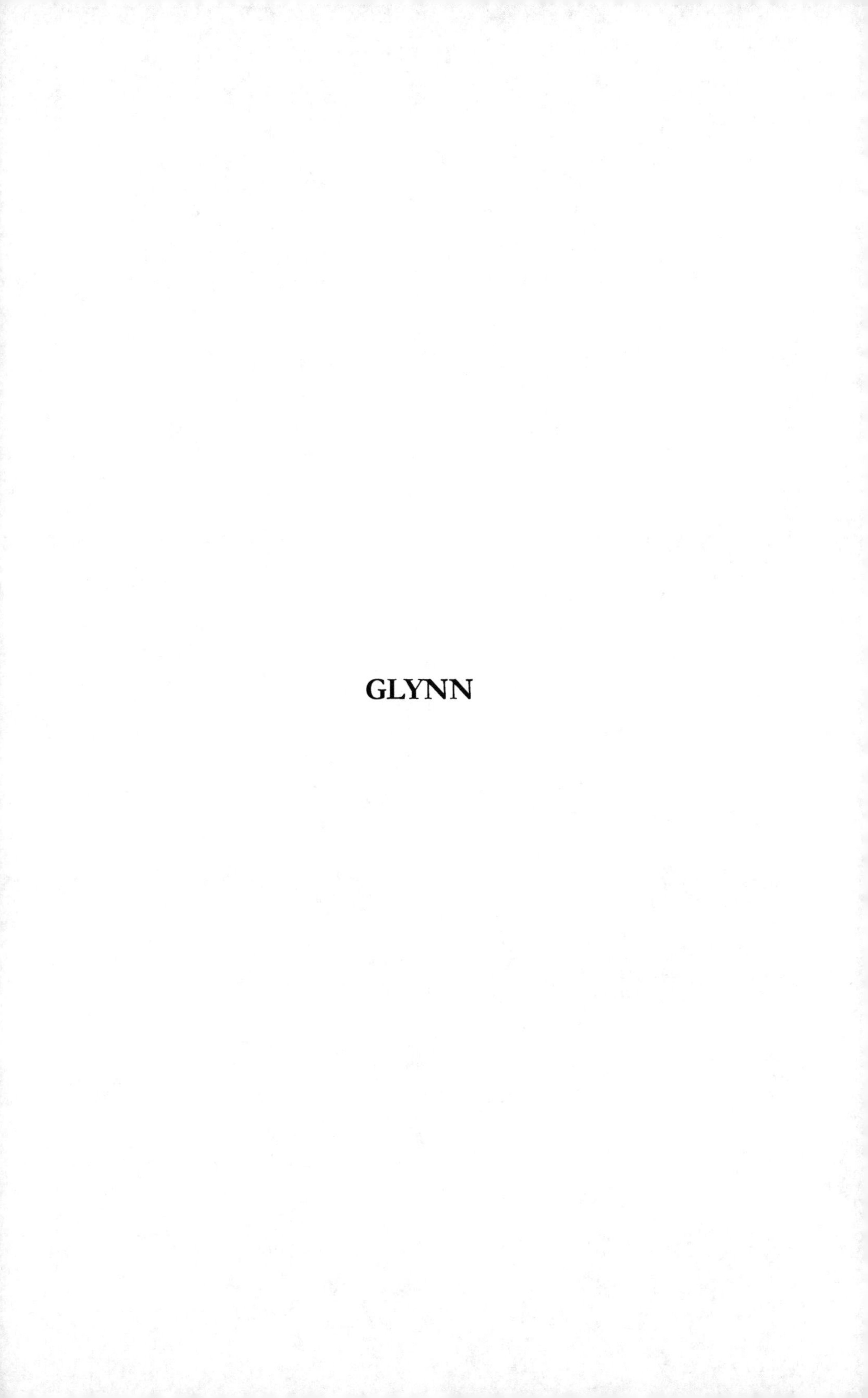

GLYNN

Walking the Dog

It was while we walked the dog;
seemed almost nothing at the time.

An evening wind
spattered sidewalk and grass with rain.
I held an umbrella;
then you were holding it too,
your wrist touching mine.
We were strangers still.

Your pup, who would not piss
for the strangeness of rain and company,
padded in under the arch we made.

We were facing each other then,
"intimate," I said.

Warmth

As I drove to work
all at once the heat came on
warm as morning covers

about the time I noticed
roadside hyacinth, daffodils
and over distant pastures
red-budding maple
the heat came on

as the Mormon Tabernacle Choir sang
"Long Time Ago"
sweet as a spring morning
and warm as last night's loving
about that time
all at once
warmth came.

Flight Home

The half moon this harvest time
travels home with me, companionably,
with a movement exactly my own,

but obscure
until I caught her first glint
off a pond
miles beneath my little window
on the darkening world.

Now she beacons every pond,
stream, lake and pool on our path.
She borrows light from the sun,
the streams and ponds from her.

I, too, must reflect
something of her sun
with the orbs of my understanding,
linked as I am in this luminous
chain of being.

Valentine

I'd like
to see your creativity,
to taste it,
to catch its scent,
to listen in, and
with full sense to feel
the way you do.

I'd like to see through eyes
I've only seen reflections from,
and taste with tongue
I've only listened to,
and listen with the sorts of ears
that silently absorb the wave
of the crashing world
upon their curving strands,
and feel at last the
waterfall of feeling you've absorbed.

Take this in
as you take
the world; make
no mistake—
your mind I'd see
with all its wondrous
twists and turns of
sensibility and sense.

The Challenge (of a fairy tale)

My princess, seated atop her glass hill,
taunts me with epithets and a challenge:
clown, court jester, page—fool,
scale my throne with your mounts,
the gold, the white, and the black,
take my golden apples three,
survey my kingdom from the topmost turret,
ride with me the meadows and the hills,
chase the foxes from their dens.

Walk the red carpet
and drink with me in daily ritual
from the fountain of youth.

Blossoms

She grows and brings in blossoms
whenever the spreading gray-green
threatens to blank color from life,
bright orange towers of sun star
a spiky red pinwheel of bromeliad
on the dark red-flowered tablecloth this morning,
tulips, white, red, and orange in the garden,
a bush replete with yellow "daisies,"
and the purple-robed locust in full bloom.
A green, full-branching rose bush
hasn't yet gotten the message,
and this morning she
is dressed all in brown,
letting her flowers, trees and bushes blossom,
for now.

Goddess of Blossoms

The pinion still sparkle
with what's left of last night's shower.
The fogged windowpane sparkles with rain drops.

Having risen from sleep the goddess of blossoms
arranges vases and flowers on the sunroom table,
purple tulips, pink and yellow orchids,
and tall roses, pink and yellow,
set in a narrow, bronze-wrapped vase,
a man and a woman in small sculpture
under the towering roses,
arms wide to embrace.

Touch and Such

Must you make beautiful all you touch?
The bouquet of flowers and plants in pots,
arrangements of stone, shell and conch,
a still life of Mexican pottery on the sideboard,
shawls draped on dressers,
your dress so various,
your hair, the sweet disorder, pin and weave.

Not to mention the little biographies,
reports, emails to family, storied syllabi;
a story to help mother across,
a letter to bring brother John
the life he might own.

Not to mention your caresses,
a hundred times a hundred to make me whole.

Cold Hands

Cold hands upon your breasts—
"Warm those hands somewhere else."

Honey that's not what you want,
my hands in other places,
exploring other Tetons, other faces.

Gracious slopes alive,
get your wits about you;
it's only here I wish to warm
my hands—not flout you.

Welcome my embraces,
my strokes in other places,
caressing hills and valleys too,
exploring what your face is.

It's only you I would adore,
all parts of you forever,
now and evermore.

The Song of Longing and Love

When the pain is at its worst
after the brief but savage exchange
propelled by weightier crises of age
and others of our making—
when the pain is in flood
it's time to stop at the grocers
to buy makings for rich salads,
time to accept the dog bone
she offers in fun on the way home.
And as the road curves around the sparkling city,
descending to the home set just off the arroyo,
time to listen again to the "Song Without Words,"
the song of longing and love.

Old Wounds

After the old wounds are opened,
and pain streams,
the heart opens to receive.

Iconography of a Gold Ring

Nicked a bit at the edges,
bent a little out of round,
worn these 18 years.

Once regular patterns
are now hieroglyphics
we know by heart.

Two thin rings of black
define three rings of gold,
burnished and growing year by year,
trinity of love,
body, spirit, and soul.

The Worth of an Occupied Space

Were it not for you,
the space you occupy
would be lonesome as a cowboy's lament,
numb as a hammered thumb,
absent as a severed limb,
silent as the tomb—
the space you occupy
is a moveable feast
for the eyes light captured
in a thousand prisms—the space
you occupy.

Were it not for that special space,
displacing lament, numbness, absence,
silence, and the dark—
what would replace the vacuum
none of us, not nature herself,
could tolerate?

Sleeping Beauty

The sun rises and the morning blossoms,
cumuli against the blue sky,
roses on the trellis and bushes
by the bundle opening to the sun,
delicate pink, bright yellow, deep red, coral,
yellow petals blown to grace the gravel.

Quiet under the star-pointed night
in the glow of its homes,
the pastoral valley still sleeps
before the sun touches it to life.

Stretching to the Jemez Mountains,
the distant valley wakes with the morning sun.

And you, sleeping beauty,
on the day of your birth
wake to the rising sun.

Serenity

I look upon her face
sculpted equally by thought and passion.
We are lying together.

Her face registers peace,
not pain nor troubles past,
but a passionate serenity.

We are lying together,
congruent, as if a sculptor
had made each for each.

Two Birthdays—to Remember

Going into, and out of, our seventies, don't forget
the genes that took our mothers into their nineties;
the graces that have given us health,
faces pleasant to look upon,
and talents by the dozen.

Don't forget that fortune
has gifted us 27 years
we didn't necessarily deserve;
that like the old lady we know what it's like
to live in a shoe, but also in beautiful homes
we've shaped to our liking.

And more fortunate
that in this wide world
we found each other, and—
through sickness and health, thick and thin—
have each other. And

Jinja, where we sit and talk
and bring it all together
with Shaking Beef and Manhattans—
don't forget that booth
as precious as a purchased pew.

Helen Leaving
(mother and daughter)

After her daily bathing in the stream of love,
cascades of kisses over her face,
neck and shoulders, arms and breast;
after the talks and stories,
her daughter, the wind,
while the Whippoorwill sounded his five notes
and the crickets sang,
came whispering through the screens into her house
and nudged open her bedroom door,
like a Sheltie, insistent.
Then curling around her, the sun warm on leaves
and the sky blue with silver clouds streaming like hair,
the wind asked for her breath,
and she gave it.

ENVIRONMENT

For Now

No humans walked the Jemez Mountains,
forty-thousand years ago
when the caldera exploded for the last time,
heaving the mountains aloft,
scattering earth and rock for a hundred miles,
and spreading lava tens of feet thick
for dozens of miles in every direction.

Lucky the Jemez had settled down
by the time humans walked across from Asia.

Luckier still the land began to warm and blossom,
welcoming them to a new world
of meadow and mountain, forest, grassy plain,
abundant wildlife, fruit and grain,
as if a benevolent God knew they were coming.

"Go forth, go forth and multiply," etc, which they did,
the only impediments rogue volcanoes, earthquakes
here and there, a few hurricanes, floods and droughts.

And lately, quietly, over all the world,
deserts and oceans creeping up on them—
but nothing blowing them to smithereens,
nothing, nothing at all.

Drought, Summer 2012

No. No!
Didn't see it coming this summer.
Yeah, had a bad one in the 50s.
Never thought we'd see *that* again.
Well yeah, 30s also, but just the plains.
Yeah, global warming, you never know;
every heat wave, flood, tornado, hurricane
has it own causes.
So many now, so widespread?
Each to his own.
We're OK where I live.

Fire

Nero fiddles, Rome burns.
We fiddle, the Planet begins to burn—
decade by decade with multiple severity:
North America, South America, Siberia, Asia,
Europe.

Imagine the sight from space,
as our burn-prone planet picks up the pace.
Grey-white over blue, gold scorching brown,
Then black and blue,
after Apollo is through with her,
and perforce the human race.

Flood

It's not only our low-lying islands
flooding while we fumble,
but all our great and beautiful seaside cities.
Let me mention by name a few: Venice, London
Shanghai, Mumbai, Calcutta, Singapore, Manila,
Osaka, New Orleans, New York, Miami, Los Angeles,
Buenos Aires, Rio de Janeiro; and first to go, Dhaka (Bangladesh,
lest we forget).

Comprehend? Of course not.
Imagine? Actuality outstrips imagination every decade:
glaciers going, going—gone within decades;
Greenland, with every measurement
melting faster than expected;
six-hundred and seventy-five cubic miles
of the Western Arctic Ice Sheet
melting, irrevocably, faster than expected.

The Dutch, with educated imaginations,
are preparing for a sea rise of two and a half feet by 2050.
Half the above-mentioned cities will then be in flood,
for which we are not preparing.

By 2100 expect, oh, a three or four foot rise in sea,
perhaps more, our seashores drowning with their cities,
for which we have no imagination—or preparation.

Should the West Arctic ice sheet and Greenland
continue to melt in concert, expect a thirty-foot rise in sea.
Can you imagine? Not yet.
Not yet will be too late in a decade.

You fathers who rule the planet,
you with dear sons and daughters,
grandsons and granddaughters—
imagine your global sins
inflicting punishment upon all children
to the third and fourth generation,
and beyond.

Picture the calculated rise in sea,
all the ice going, going—gone,
the Statue of Liberty up to her waist,
hills peaking above the western ocean,
the Flood, without rain, rising silent.

Cascadia Fault—Catastrophes

We don't believe in some future catastrophe
any more than death,
our minds perfectly tuned to denial.
Others will be swept away,
not us, not I.
Others will die.

No need to prepare; it's not happening.
The news thick with tragedy—our catharsis.

Overhead, out to sea, in the wild, it's happening.
Deep under the Northwest Coast continental pressure
builds to a long-delayed release.

The guillotine suspends above,
the block rests below.
With the click of release
the end will not be slow.

Life Afar

The games we play against our vast universe,
as if to save our sorry selves from ourselves,
discover a new earth light years distant,
that perhaps proves fecund,
produces the likes of us,
in a billion years or so,
begins again the merry-go-round.

Our current neighborhood playground—
Mars, most likely a one way ticket
to see if a select bunch might
get along with themselves,
send back a blueprint
as to how it's done in isolation
on a dead planet.

Sandy, a Song for the Planet

From Staten Island to Cape May Beach,
the Jersey Shore is quite a reach,
a beautiful beach—but not any more;
Sandy came in and took the shore.

I take my own;
you might have known.

The beach had houses, cars and boats,
neighborhoods full of stuff that floats.
She marched right in, gave them a lift,
rearranged the lot, set them adrift.

My ocean is warm;
time to erase the norm.

Polar bears have lost their beach,
ice of course, now that's a reach.
Lost their life rafts, ice as well;
warming comes within the swell.

I take my own;
you must have known.

The tundra, the tundra has methane in store,
all along the Arctic shore.
The tundra is melting, now that's a scare.
The methane will rise, beware.

My oven's this zone.
Game's over when it's grown.

Universally speaking the earth's a small place,
a tiny blue gem in the vastness of space.
Pinpoint far planets, search as you must;
so far we've got rocks, ice, and dust.

Tend her, this Eden we own.
Tend her, she is home.

Back at the Shore

They're building again, preparing my dinner;
the width of their memory couldn't be slimmer.
You can count on my coming, though the date isn't set.
You've set the table for the supper-not-yet.

Oh humans, greedy humans,
take only your own;
I take what's been on loan.

Oakwood Beach

During the year gone by, the state
has pulled its head from the sand,
offering, in the deepening, disconsolate dusk, escape;
but block on block isolate porch lights
brave a relentless ocean.

Pull your planted feet from the sand;
console your fortunate selves.
You might have been swept out to sea,
or drowned in your basements.

Console yourselves, put out the lights.
Walk while you still have footing,
while—high and hungry sea on its way—
you have a chance to plant elsewhere,
saving yourselves, your sons and daughters,
grandsons and granddaughters,
who most certainly will find the floodwaters
kicking in the door, blowing out the windows,
and punching out at last the remaining lights.

Tumbleweeds

Where the earth's been disturbed
the tumbleweeds grow,
prickling, stickling, rootless,
wandering where the wind sends them—
over the range, into arroyos,
up against fences, casitas, and barns.

Where the earth has been scraped of its grasses
tumbleweeds take over,
real estate to stake out and make their own.

Grasses are growing at the roots of dead tumbleweed,
silent and green in the shade of grey tumbleweed.
Land grab's for the rootless.

The grasses wait.
The earth will be theirs.

Neuroscientists Take a Trip Down the River

We are rafting the San Juan, Glen Canyon,
attempting to calculate the difference between
wading into the digital deluge
and floating down the river,
nature's stream of consciousness.

We spent the night at Recapture Lodge,
launched at Mexican Hat.
Once under the high bridge we lost
all electronics to the river's flow.
The trash emptied we could attend
to the circling hawks, the vistas around the next bend,
the rapids, the ripples, the big horn sheep,
the narrow canyons we hiked—the silence.

The third day, time slowing to the river's crawl,
ideas woke from their graves.
This seminal study—could people learn better
after a walk in the woods rather than the street?
a float on the river rather than wading the digital deluge?
Could persons with digital fatigue find full potential?
What happens to the brain as it rests?

We pulled out, neglecting our watches, emails, and coffee.
We recommend down time, listening, engaging,
avoiding distractions digital and otherwise.
And from the heart of silence, returned to our studies.

Love Lost

Under the overcast lurching left and right
into a blustering northeast-northwest wind,
driving through the West Texas oil fields,
mourning the loss to come;
mile after mile under grey sky
and a featureless landscape, mourning.

For the news is bad, and worse by the week.
The great West Arctic Ice sheet melting irrevocably,
the furnace and flood to come,
at once baking the planet and drowning
our seaside civilizations one by one.

Noah will not build us an ark.
Daniel will not save us from the furnace.
Elijah will not supplicate for rain.

How do we mourn the only home
we ever—will ever own?

Gershwin floats on this morning's airwaves.
"Bess, you is my woman now."
Now, for a day or so—then never.
This is how we mourn love lost, forever.

Mind Set

We humans are bent for extinction
having set the stage:
the planet succumbing to fever;
nuclear arsenals in place;
a President Elect to begin the Last Act,
turn the page.

On the sixth day of Creation,
(humans not yet in sight),
You could have rested,
having made the loon, the swan,
the hummingbird, geese in flight.

Earth Song

When our meadows and forests succumb to the deserts,
our lakes and our marshes, their fountains vanishing,
lift the last mists with the sighs of their dying,
where will we find our oasis?

Our vast Ozone canopy shudders and rends wide.
The life giving sun strikes our crops and our krill,
and scorches our genes with a deadly radiation.
Where will we fly from this furnace?

Doomsday you say—is our fate so appalling?
The fields are still green, trees bud in the spring,
and the robin returns; the sky is not falling.

All through the country the warblers are dying,
the orioles, hummingbirds, tanagers, thrushes,
while blue jays and crows,
the nest robbers and scavengers,
gather like locusts
and cut the still air with shrill cries.

Who will cancel these signs?
Who will sing for us now?

Who give us gold when the monarch has fluttered its last?
Who grow meadows and fields when weeds hold sway?
Who breed of roaches the vanishing species of mammals?

What world will be ours
when ours is the furnace we fire,
when we are the swarm all devouring,
when we rend the blue heaven
and summon the sun as our curse?
In the backwash of our rockets every dusky sparrow fell—
gods, now, of earth and sky,
whose eye is on the sparrow,
in the morning mist chirping for spring,
the sun-inspired respiring
of our expiring earth?

Clothed in aqua
earth rises in space
over a beaten moonscape canopied with night—
and beckons our return.

The Bent Planet (for John Kerry)

Our bent is discord.

Yet, hostility permeating the air,
members of the Chicago Symphony,
hurling expletives from section to section—
when it came to the score before them,
filled Orchestra Hall with exquisite harmony.

Maestros, set the scores before us;
take up the batons; draw from us music
that will make us weep,
listening to harmonies that neither nature
nor the universe could have imagined.

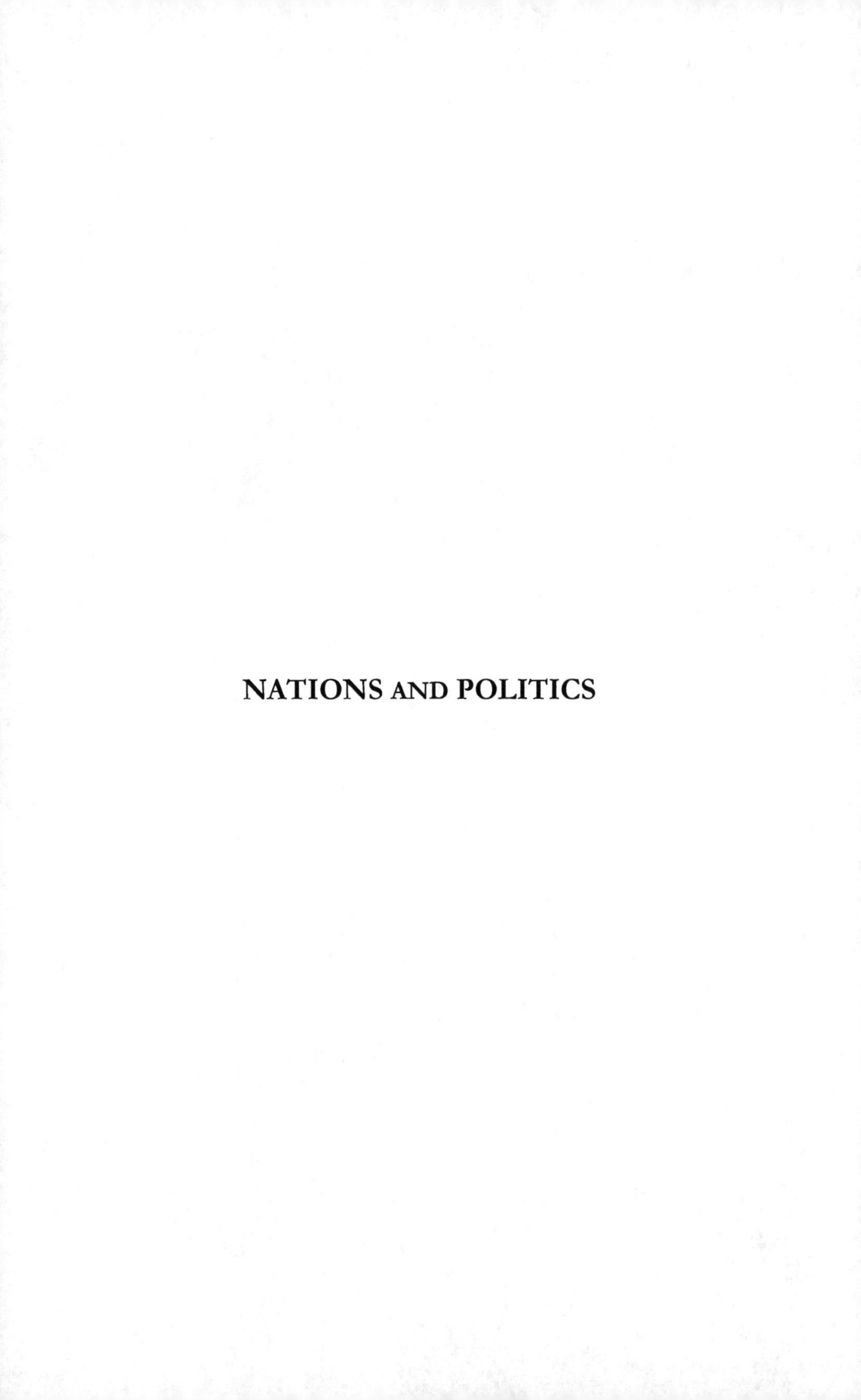

NATIONS AND POLITICS

Newfoundland

Newfoundland,
split from three continents,
island alone.
Stand off from us.
Shroud your cliffs;
let no new world nor old find your secret,
your poorhouse treasure.

Cold, storm-ringed beauty,
first found and abandoned,
welcome no new lovers to your coves.
Give up your mines.
Sacrifice if you must your wilderness.
Offer them instead your oceans.

But keep close your treasures:
the music your women lift
talking among themselves;
the courage of one man
stolid upon the winter ocean.

The ceremonies of morning and evening
in your coves.

Keep them from your poorhouse treasures,
lest your diamond store crush to sand,
your cliffs crumble.

Emperors, Kings, Potentates, Dictators, and Such

Why would anyone think these were a good idea?
Israel, put out with Samuel's wicked sons,
said, give us a king to rule, like the other nations.

Samuel said, let me check with the Lord.
The Lord said, bad idea, knowing slavery was in store,
and poverty. Well, they said,
we want one anyway.

Samuel, you remember,
the mild-mannered adolescent,
who couldn't believe it was the Lord,
calling him again and again to serve justice
to the People of Israel,
which he did all his life.

Never mind, they wanted kings.
We've got kings, and potentates, and emperors,
and dictators by the dozens—it's a shame
the Quakers showed up so late, a shame that
the "inner light" had to be Fat Boy bursting overhead,
hotter than ten-thousand suns and spreading death
everywhere the wind went.

Potentates and nation states?
Let's try " The Baltic Way,"
an unbroken chain six hundred kilometers long,
Estonians, Latvians, and Lithuanians, two million
hand in hand, for freedom.

Let it be Estonia,
singing in its schools,
and singing for its soul—
three-hundred-thousand voices strong,
while the occupying nation looked on.

Let it be the peoples of Tunisia, Egypt, Bahrain,
Libya, Yemen, Sudan, and Syria,
laying down their lives for their friends.

And let it be Mohammed Bouazizi,
the Tunisian fruit cart vender,
who preferred death to a slap in the face,
and set himself—and the Mideast—afire.

Rump.gov

Trump is rumping for President;
what do you think of that?
He wears an air of confidence;
he wears a baseball cap.

He's got a rack of baseball bats;
his choice of use is random,
radically random in fact.
He swings them with abandon.

He's greater than greats can be,
greater than anyone is he;
greater than greats long past.
How long will Trumpling last?

Pig-eye now is President;
what do you think of that?
Wears less that air of confidence;
still wears that baseball cap.

Preliminary Study

Clearly, the world is falling to ruin,
though statistical evidence is incomplete.
Consider evidence from early researchers:
"Things fall apart;
the center cannot hold." [1]

This popular study assesses
four thousand years of world history,
drawing heavily upon material from the occult
and first hand observation.

"A crowd flowed over London Bridge so many
I had not thought death had undone so many." [2]
The naïveté of the observer is noteworthy,
the language again unscientific.
However, the techniques of head counting
and pedestrian mapping, though primitive,
have been used by subsequent researchers,
similar conclusions resulting.

"When you come, as you soon must,
to the streets of our city,
mad-eyed from stating the obvious . . ." [3]

This assessment envisions a nuclear catastrophe,
the obliteration of symbols such as deer and oaks
by which we have known ourselves.

A profusion of recent research
is marked by the absence of method and restraint.
Consider.
Several hundreds mass tonight before the oracle.
He arranges a miscellany of papers, books, and notebooks;
calms himself and us with harmonium and mantra,
and begins the long, random litany of devastations.
The crowd is pleased;
no one troubles his lines with weeping.
Yet no one is deceived;
each sees his world in shambles.

The oracle sees the happy, devastated audience.
He is pleased and concerned; he offers
solutions: "Come," he quavers,
"into my shelter of grass and I will give you love,
and ease your troubled mind." [4]

---

[1] W. B. Yeats, "The Coming."
[2] T. S. Eliot, "The Wasteland"
[3] Richard Wilbur, "Advice to a Prophet"[4]
[4] Allen Ginsberg, at Northwestern University

TrampTrumpTramp (Sestina)

We've lost ourselves to insanity,
our politics to heretics,
our logic to magic.
Reason's out of season,
sense, nonsense,
reality, banality.

Can we ban banality,
banish insanity,
beat nonsense,
burn heretics,
give reason a season,
let logic trump magic?

Wands for magic,
flags for banality,
balloons every season,
cheers for insanity,
welcome heretics
at the podium of nonsense.

Speak to us nonsense,
confound us with magic,
make sacred the heretic,
up with banality,
up with insanity,
mindless the season.

Go with the season,
dance with nonsense,
play with insanity,
trick us with magic,
drum beat banality,
parade the heretic.

Out with the heretic,
out with the season,
banish banality,
sense erase nonsense,
light expose magic,
sanity, insanity.

Away with banality, nonsense,
heretics, the season,
magic, insanity.

A New Day for Columbus: Border Town Boom

Selling like hot cakes, says agent Skinner (former mayor),
houses bought for cash,
new Lincolns and Cadillacs on the streets,
with hubcaps worth more than a truck.

"Well, where did they get this money?" Skinner questions.
"Here we make about fifteen-thousand a year."

"Criminals don't live here," says Maria,
owner of the of the Poncho Villa Café.
"It's serene here.
It's tranquil here."

Meanwhile, Columbus's ever changing
police force of four
sits at the shack they call home.
"We know the names of these people;
they'll do jail time," says Angelo Viga, the new Chief,
gas fumes occasionally curling at the door.
"Let's go down to Villa's for a smoke."

Another Day

Who would have guessed?—another raid;
but not Poncho Villa and six hundred friends,
just a few guys from the Bureau of Alcohol, Tobacco,
Firearms, and Drug Enforcement Administration.
Arrested the mayor, police chief, a trustee
and eight others on drugs and weapons charges.
The guys with Lincolns and Cadillacs—gone.

Goldman Sachs

Sacks of red spring wheat,
bought them cheap,
held them, wheat got scarce
around the world.
Held them, demand got rich;
the poor went hungry—
and starved.

Fat cats, Sachs, harvesting gold by the bushel;
the ancient prophets have words for you and your wives:
"Cows of Bashen, who oppress the poor
and crush the destitute;"
you will be "carried straight out
and pitched on the dung hill."
That's what Amos said.

"You hate good and love evil;
you flay men alive
and tear the very flesh from their bones;
you devour the flesh of my people."
That's what Micah said.

You've got barns full of golden wheat.
Someone's going to get what's left of your soul.
Jesus, that's what Jesus said.

Republican Politicos 21st C.

Rampant insanity—where
are the snake pits when
we need them most,
pythons and boa constrictors
when constriction is urgent,
rattlesnakes to give notice of impending strike,
black mambas for the swift, deadly strike,
king cobras to finish off what's left,
coral snakes to deaden lies left twitching.

Prophets forecast the destruction of Earth,
all we hold dear
calling to account you Atheists,
who believe in yourselves alone,
leaving Earth to its fate.

Prophets of Baal,
offering our children to the fire;
expect visitation before you expire.
Hell's fires won't wait.

The Mideast

Here's to the muggers, goons, thugs,
torturers, murderers, slugs.

Here's to the peoples, steeples of hope,
who have given the nations their scope.

Sent the murderers back to their lairs;
sent the Pharaohs packing, those purveyors of lies.

May the cries of the martyrs run deep,
waking in every nation the fault lines,
so long asleep.

Tahrir Square

The doves are making congress
upon the power lines.
Their grasp is firm,
their lineage ancient,
beast-footed Theropods,
cousins to Tyrannosaurus Rex.

Line upon line they perch,
speaking peace among themselves,
speaking peace to power.

The Time of our Lives

It was a spectacular view
from the summit of Lenin Peak:
blue Lake Karakul to the east, China beyond;
Communism Peak, once Stalin's, to the southwest.

It was an historic event,
ten nations welcome (if not to the country)
to climb Lenin Peak.
The French came with Beaujolais,
the English with beards,
and the Americans to pioneer new ascents.

12,000 feet:
edelweiss,
and quiet herds of cattle sheep, and horses.
But Lenin Peak blocked the moon at night.

13,000 feet:
a tumbling mountain stream,
and a meadow bright with flowers.
But beyond, the Pass of the Travelers,
and a vast moraine of slag and sand.

17,000 feet:
an earthquake!
Sky black with massive snow
shelving off the ice cliff over our heads
and around us.

Then a search, down through blinding snow,
to Japanese and Scot's tents.
Michael, the student of economics, found the way.

Base camp again next morning.
Edelweiss, under a foot of snow,
and Gary Ullin dead under an avalanche
at the Nineteenth Party Congress Peak.

Russians that day found three Estonians
dead on the east face of Lenin Peak,
and two injured, who later died.
To the Peak again!
Three of us tried the direct route
up the northeast ridge.
After 2,000 feet we turned back
fearing another avalanche.

Next day we pushed again for the summit.
A storm caught us
and we heard thunder in the clouds below.
We camped at 19,000 feet.

After resting a day in storm
we pushed to the summit ridge.
At 22,000 feet the shrieking hurricane held us
two nights, three, we never knew,
tore at us and snapped the tent down in spite.
But morning came clear and cold.

Now for the summit,
the last, steep snow face! But there,
stretched on snow and rock against the sky,
a body. Then one by one six more Soviet women,
professional climbers all, frozen.
"Come down immediately, have courage,"
said the voice through the hurricane.
"Goodbye," they said, "we will die."

It was a spectacular view
from the summit of Lenin Peak:
blue Lake Karakul to the east, China beyond,
Communism Peak once Stalin's to the southwest.
But we were anxious to descend
and marked seven bodies with willow wands
off the first slope.

Hawks

Morning, jets from the air force base
leave a fan of contrails,
bisecting to A's and V's and X's
spreading to swaths of burnt gas.

Must be a lark to streak the sky
leaving crisscross notice of your fun.

Over Rio en Medio a Hawk
circles gracefully leaving no trace
of the pure pleasure of a morning's sail.

On the Knoll

At dusk I sit with my golden rescue pup
on a knoll across the valley from Los Alamos,
the sun turning pink the undersides of grey cumuli,
a half-moon on edge keeping watch.

On the distant mesa lights begin to twinkle,
strung like strands of DNA
or a compacted, fractured Milky Way.

I think of the scientists
hustled up the canyon in utmost secrecy,
housed in shacks and Quonset Huts
to make the instruments that in a flash
turned two cities to ash,
in those moments out of mind
the threat to human kind.

Assemble!

Walked down the road
to get the Sunday paper
hoping to fuse current news
and my view of Los Alamos
without tempting fission.

Wicked powers dissemble
to disassemble our nucleus,
split Union—assemble!

Force lies in fusion.
Save the Race, save Union, and more
before we are unsheathed like an onion,
nothing left in store.

POEMS HERE AND THERE

Marigolds

Two and two are four; four and four are eight;
Eight and eight are sixteen . . .
Inchworm, inchworm, measuring the marigolds . . .
- "Inchworm," by Frank Loesser

The marigolds have jumped
their circumscribed pots, seeding
themselves in colorful disarray
along the flagstone pathway,
refusing to be encircled or measured
by rule or inchworm—
how beautiful they are
splashing the pea gravel
with petals red and orange and yellow,
nestling against the Ruby Cundra
and under the young rose bushes,
who cannot hold a candle
to these little coals holding fire
late into autumn—how
beautiful they are beyond measure.

Hibiscus in the Sun Room

Each morning, sun rising,
with one blossom glorious rich pink,
the Hibiscus blesses us with its bounty
from our nearest star,
proclaiming its singular beauty,
here, now, just once.

Frost

Sap trapped in the cold.
Gold leaves and orange and red,
autumn leaves hanging out
or drifting, as these from the ash
to clad the ground—
nature's last green is red, orange, and gold.

Death of a Sheltie

Death is absence,
disembodied memories,
not the living, breathing intelligence,
but memories that leap—
two small paws and a stretch—
upon the thigh.

Memories only
of the muzzle nudging
and nudging again when the stroking stopped.

Of pirouettes for the pleasures
of "eat" and "walk,"
and all the squirrels he never caught.

Of fierce herding,
hard on the shoulders of dogs
three times his size chasing sticks.

Of the barks that shepherded our distance,
and when the argument was pitched,
a wet lick for each.

Of the face behind the darkened glass expectant of return.

We return to the house bereft of that face
and the scrape of small paws;
return to memories
of days saturated with pain,

when only a turn of his head
and a flick of his eyes
acknowledged our tears.

Yes, we are weeping,
for absence is hard upon us.
That living, breathing being
took leave with a twist
of time before and after
that we cannot bend
our minds to comprehend.

Santa Fe

The mountains fold like fur,
silver fox at sunrise,
red fox at sunset.

The sky glows rose
long before sunrise strikes the hills,
long after sunset releases them.

Morning and evening the Ortiz mountains,
scissor-cut silhouettes,
stand stark against the Sandias.

No longer high-minded, cumuli love the mountains,
settle upon the peaks,
nestle in the gorges,
lie low with the valleys.

The wind loves what's left of the rocks,
sweeping up the dust, a bridegroom wild with desire,
sweeping with abandon over hill, house and roadway,
oblivious to all things civilized.

After wind and rain
all that's left is the pungency of cedar and juniper
permeating still air.

Day after day bright blue sky
brings us heaven
as palpable as breath.

Mount Holyoke College, Thanksgiving

Morning fog filters through the bare branches
of giant oaks and elms
and brushes the brownstone face
of the stained glass cathedral, Forbes Library,
just one of the sanctuaries
gracing this glade made campus.

A mist brushes the beautiful brownstones
where we sit in perfect privilege
to entertain the world beyond.

Who set these foundations,
laid the cornerstones,
fashioned the intricate stained glass,
sculpted the granite window frames,
hauled and laid the bricks,
built the towers, laid the floors,
shaped the great wooden arches?

Where are those who for a hundred years
have given our minds such sanctuary?

Just outside our gothic classroom window,
as if summoned,
stocky workmen in tan overalls and plaid shirts rise to view
on the railed platform of a giant lift.

I walk to the window and open it
in all good humor to welcome them.
"Sorry," one says, before I can apologize
for the professorial presence exclusive
of these founding fathers,
or invite them in.

A Concert for Victims of an Earthquake

In Chicago at the Lyric
they are making concert for the living,
while by hundreds your bodies lie crushed,
your voices stifled under stones
once raised with hearty cries.

In Chicago, under rain that falls
from somber skies this Sunday afternoon,
we raise these strains
passionate for resurrection.

Rescue

She called 911 off the edge of scree
on Old Baldy, called again and again.

The sixth time she got through.
They got coordinates, sent a helicopter
made for such a rescue,
a pilot made for the same,
and a spotter.

Her boyfriend was up ahead somewhere—
a little argument perhaps?
"I'm going ahead to get us out of here."
"Fine."

The copter came in, landed under a lowering, leaden sky.
They walked half a mile to find her,
walked her back, exhausted, cold,
strapped her in, lifted off, snow falling and darkness,
nicked the tail rotor on a rock or a lone tree
a quarter mile up, cart-wheeled a quarter mile down,
threw pilot and passenger on the rocks.

Spotter, leg crushed, back broken, went to find her,
dead, but couldn't reach his pilot.
They called to each other through the night,
then silence.
Morning, he hobbled a mile to rescue.

Massifs, Everest, K2, Rainier,
a thousand of your kind
offer a cold shoulder
to the thoughtless novice and expert alike.
And to those who would rescue,
slabs for sacrifice.

Stepping into Danger—the Twilight Zone

It's called the California 200,
a twilight desert ritual, 40-mile track barely marked
over arroyo, hills, mounds, range and piles of rock
with souped up super trucks suspended for flight.

It's a party, a celebration of the wild remote—
and they're off, headlights searching
tail lights through clouds of dust,
hittin' 80 on the straights.

And we're off to the rock pile
to watch them go airborne.
We crowd five feet from the track—never mind
the 100-foot rule; closer is better.
Step up to the track, share the danger,
smell it—here comes Mr. Sloppy (that's right);
he's in the air, sidewise,
and we can feel danger to the bone
as he plants all fours on the ground
and rolls over us a hundred feet
right to where we should have stood.

Look! It's an off-civilization celebration of the wild—
we've left a memorial: a sneaker, a cap,
dusty sunglasses, and a desert-wood cross.

Accident

He stands on top of the dam
looking across the reservoir to the knob
where the cabin will rise
by pine at the water's edge.

The dam face falls twenty feet behind him.
Vines and bushes root in cracks and ledges.
Here and there water seeps through
and down the dam's dark, smallpox face.

He once imagined himself falling,
but controlled, sliding,
cuts and bruises only.

But his thoughts are constructive;
he's going to build a cabin.

All day for a campsite
he cut down the saplings,
felling dead elm and ash into the gulch
while they watched, his boys
and a woman. In the heat of it
he ran with the knee-thick trunk of a falling ash,
dropping it upon the growing pile
of saplings and brush.

The day done he stands upon the dam
barefoot, in trunks, and reaches down
for the dead elm, unsightly,
stuck in the spillway.

New Moon By Half

Kneeling, he grasps the bone-white branch.
Just lever it over and down.
He stands and strains, the branch a bow.
You're—then the crack—doing it.
And he remembers his imagined fall.
In midair over the scar face,
cold as stone the thought,
now you're doing it.

The dam's first statement, adamant,
cracks his imagination.
His mind bows,
shuts down the sensitive receptors.
He does not feel how reluctantly
the dam lets him fall
before its message is complete.

The knee is ripped,
the feet gashed he knows
only the half of it.
Get on top again.

He walks upon the dam
tracking blood to the spillway,
sits, and washes his gashes.
He cannot hear the fracture talking
or imagine an infected joint.

I'll get it sewed up, he thinks,
and be back in a week or so.

The reservoir is quiet,
keeping its secrets beneath a mirror surface
under the declining sun.

Coronary Artery Bypass
(for brother Jim, heart surgeon)

Why all this bother!
This exhaustive, meticulous labor
for a senseless mass of beef,
this scrubbed and swabbed plumber,
this scared and faulty heart?

But there!
The incision, neck to sternum end;
thumbnail deep muscle layered red and white;
blood trickling into the long, narrow channel;
suction nozzle swiping, snuffling;
from the crackle of the cauterizing Bovee
acrid smoke rising.

And there!
In the thigh, two deep gashes;
a kinky, white vein is uprooted inch by inch
from its bed of red muscle
and resinous, bubbly fat.

Two at the thigh,
four at the chest,
one at the heart lung machine,
two at the head attending the sleeper's sleep;
one circulating, one supervising, one watching.
And beyond the doors a company:
samplers, testers, sterilizers, records keepers,
analyzers, cooks—why all this

bother, this exhausting labor, this
the bone saw now, gripped firm . . .
For a moment only this hours-long,
second-by-second operation hesitates.
"You have to step on the peddle,
all the way down."
The sternum unzips like a jacket.
Through the scent of alcohol
smoke again rises.

Now the spreader, primitive as a pipe wrench,
cranks open the chest cavity.
The pale, grey-blue heart's sack
emerges in motion,
mask of the heart beat.

Careful, careful, now cut it open
and stretch it like skins to the spreader.
Why all this

there, beating, beating,
in its smooth, white chamber,
in its sanctuary . . .

He slides his right hand,
his broad plumber's hand,
under the heart
and holds it.

Fernando's Restaurant

Six months ago his mother got cancer
and died in the prime of her age.
I ask him tonight how he's doing, he answers,
I'm ok, but eighty's too early
to turn the page.

With hardly a pause he gets his guitar
finds a chair and sits very close.
Then plays without stopping it seems for an hour
in the glow of that life he supposed
was to last for an age.

He plays Requerdos remembering her life,
intensity lining his face;
he plays the classics without ever stopping,
then stands, his guitar at his side,
and we share an embrace.

Six months ago his mother got cancer,
and died in the prime of her age.
Tonight he's translated his love into lyric.
He imagines she's singing, I'll wager,
a smile on her face.

The Living

Those of us "among the living"
lucky enough to be so far immortal
who cannot conceive of death
but as absence

those of us
who daily raise to half-life
the inconceivably dead

those of us
who have so far escaped
war genocide random cancers strokes
the lottery of accident
by a foot a finger a hair's breadth

who wake day after day
assured of the
next
moment
which

Saying Goodbye

No one wants to say goodbye,
ever.
So we stay on the phone
or linger at the door,
though there's nothing left to say,
run with the departing train
for a last wave or glimpse
until it pulls away.
Any way to put off the goodbye,
forever.

Poetry Reading

You couldn't tell whether
he was reading his poetry
or
just
talking,
except for the lift in his voice
after he left off reading.

A Very Contemporary Poetry Reading
(at the reconstructed Body Politic)

"Not fit for man or beast out there," he said,
looking over the crowd.

The window frames fit;
imagine the carpenter at his work.

"My head wears a big and floppy heart;"
with that the house broke up,
so fitting it was.

The window frames are fitting, but silent.

The windows, sashes and frames
are also raw and unfinished,
stickers still on the smudged panes.

But the windows fit.

The Body Politic sits with its back to the windows,
facing the "agitation of the sensible universe,"
the poet's plunge to "intimate intercourse
with the moon's reflection upon the water."

No ripple disturbs the surface,
the windows, sashes, and frames,
also, enchantingly still.

Mother and Daughter

The daughter sits against the pew on the aisle.
Against her sits her tall mother,
composed, dressed in dark blue,
her short, dark hair curling obediently inward.

Her daughter sits up straight as a stick,
cheeks burning pale red,
her ungovernable hair
an ambush of prickly sprigs.

Mother and Child

Mother and child on an island,
traffic constant,
oblivious cars, pickups, semis.

Her arm cups his collar bone.
His hand clasps her arm.
He looks up.

Lighthouse Beach, Dusk

The city noises dully at my back.
The lake stretches away, flat, rippled,
and is lost under a thin rim of steel gray haze;
cinder grey above, tinged purple, then yellow
rises toward a full moon,
tilted to survey the quiet.

An airliner, stately, flying level,
leaves shore under her gaze.
Nine ducks rise, form, and cross before her.
The little ripples break and bubble.
Dusk deepens.

Down the beach a Black girl sings,
though spring is only a promise, "Summertime."

Commuters

You who come to the city silent,
faces in black print yesterday;

you who come to the city silent,
grey-faced army double-timing
down passageways of reinforced concrete;

you who come to the city,
early, silent,

are far above us,

who go from the city joking:
"You didn't bring too much in the way of weather."
"Well you know me."

Who go from the city laughing:
"I see John's working downtown,
little John, back there sorting mail."

Who go from the city
gathering at every stop
a humble community.

To Valentine Vaduga Upon Complaint 628-207

Blast out of the traffic jam
bursting angry,
broadside the corner with
pure fiery pleasure and
bust straight away
past—brakes! Too late—Radar.
Everything, full, stop.

"You may get back in your car and
sit down. It's dangerous out there."
I am suddenly sane;
the law works its rote-word peace.
"Forty eight in a thirty-five zone."
Against argument, the meter:
"You're looking at it."
But I do not need the slim pointer;
my puff is punctured;
my pride lies plummet.

"Do you want to post your driver's license
or a cash bond, sir?"
"Sir," a considerate "sir,"
completes the quieting ritual,
the law exchanging,
for my madness,
a modest dignity.

What of it?

Though the world of projects knocks
at every door, taps
at each window, and thumps
along the roof—what of it?
Out the French doors flagstone,
artistically cut and laid,
looks back at me appreciatively;
the flower garden beyond blooms;
even the aspen planted with a fist for roots
has burst into full leaf;
and birdsong floats up from the arroyo
this morning on which
I've forgotten my wristwatch.

Morning

Sun quiet on the windowsill
over dusky roses yellow and orange,
a glass of orange juice,
a bowl of cut peach and blueberries,
foamed milk atop a cup of coffee,
the sorry morning news-
paper still folded.

Friday the Thirteenth

A yellow-breasted bird flew
into our living room window
full speed and fell to the ground
breast to the sky,
dead it seemed.

You picked it up,
caressed its back and wings.
I went for a box, a rag,
water and grain for a little nest.

By then its eyes were open and blinking,
though a wing was askew.
You set it in the box,
and then it flew.

Pecking Order

First come the house wrens and red crossbills,
feeding in peace.
Then the mountain bluebirds
clearing the field, fighting fiercely for seed,
after which return the wrens and crossbills.

Five blackbirds swoop in,
fighter jets scattering the flock.
Ground feed for a while,
after which return the wrens and crossbills.

Spring in the air, mourning doves
grace the field with wrens and crossbills.

Pecking order,
everyone gets theirs.
More humane than human.

Taming Tom

Was an outdoor tom
gone hours or overnight
stalking and eating birds and mice,
fighting with neighborhood toms.

Spent thousands saving that life
for more of the same,
nights out catting, the life
life was meant to be.

Sat with tom cat Connor
in the euthanizing room,
a killing urinary infection
threatening thousands more—
agonized for an hour—
"family," we said,
"expense be damned,"
went for the cure.

Presently he's in the finishing school
called House Cat,
escaping at times for a lark;
but observation, imagination and dream
now substitute for stalking and gorging.

He's as tamed as a tom can be,
observing the wild in relative tranquility.

Casita on the Mesa (time lapse)

Something substantial that wasn't there,
just air.
Something structural
materialized out of nothing,
magically, as with the wave of a wand.

Now you don't see it;
now you do.

Doesn't matter how,
only that it happened,
and here.

Perfect Day (lyric)

The cumuli stand still today;
the sun stands still as well.
It's near the end of a perfect day
and it's not too early to tell.

Past the graying clouds the sky's bright blue,
and the slow setting sun sends a golden hue.
It's as good as can be blowing leaves all say,
as good as it gets on a perfect day.

The cumuli are golden now;
the sun has flung far west.
Let night come forth with its host of stars,
and my passions lie down to rest.

First Evening Class

I said, "I can tell,
you are going to write well;
you're beginning to do it already."
You said, "What the hell,
he might teach us to spell,
even though he looks young and unsteady."

And so we progressed;
it was all for the best.
Through tangles of rhetoric we tread.
Through the cumulative sentence
you wandered with reticence;
"just keep on trying," I said.
Through subordinate phrases,
coordinate phases,
and intricate mazes of these,
with compliments flowery,
you said, "Mr. Oury,
let's move on to something else, please."

We moved but an inch;
"the paragraph's a cinch," I said;
"just keep on using the model."
You groaned, you moaned;
one came to class stoned,
with notebook, pencil and pottle.

Close reading of essay,
"relatively easy,"
I said; "just do my bidding."
Oh task spectaculus,
tougher than calculus,
said one, and he wasn't kidding.
Enough! Lest the verse
turn worse.
I mask emotions dear—
such rhyme, such meter.

What can I say
when these evenings bring such returns?
For mistakes, laughter.
For the fears of a novice,
"I'm not a student; I'm your instructor,"
a will to see it my way and to work.
For a nickel of my thoughts, a fortune of yours.

I gave you encouragement;
you gave me the sun.

Symphony—Universe

The Brain—is wider than the sky . . .
Deeper than the sea . . .
Just the weight of God
- *Emily Dickinson*

With our impractical, abstract, mathematical play
how did we ever discover its secrets?

The Universe made these minds,
minds that loved such play.

We heard notes far off,
Gained entrance to the hall,
fine-tuned our instruments,
began to learn the score,
couldn't imagine what was in store,
that we would be so in tune,
that the Universe would open to our play,
that our minds were made for this music,
that we might have come so far.

And that within this symphony
we live and move—are.

ABOUT THE AUTHOR

Scott Oury has been writing poetry for nearly five decades. He also worked as a textbook editor, earned a Master's Degree in English, and taught writing, drama, and poetry at colleges in Massachusetts, New Jersey, and Illinois. His works have included essays, poems, and articles published in journals and newspapers; and the lead essay in a book celebrating the writer C. S. Lewis. Oury is the author of *Coming to Terms with Experience through Writing*, a guide to experiential writing for both aspiring and professional writers. He currently lives and writes in Tesuque, New Mexico.

CPSIA information can be obtained
at www.ICGtesting.com
Printed in the USA
BVHW040832030419
544383BV00011B/4/P

9 780578 433707